The Toddler Book

The Toddler Book

How to Enjoy Your Growing Child

Rachel Waddilove

A Lion Book
an imprint of
Lion Hudson plc
Wilkinson House, Jordan Hill Road,
Oxford OX2 8DR, England
www.lionhudson.com
ISBN 978 0 7459 5296 3

First edition 2008
10 9 8 7 6 5 4 3 2 1 0

Acknowledgments

p. 42 Extract taken from *Children Learn What They Live* by
Dorothy Law Nolte. Used by permission of the estate of Ms Nolte.
pp. 178–79 Scripture quotation is taken from the Holy Bible,
New Living Translation, copyright © 1996. Used by permission
of Tyndale House Publishers, Inc., Wheaton, Illinois 60189.
All rights reserved.
p. 184 Scripture quotation is taken from the Holy Bible,
New International Version, copyright © 1973, 1978, 1984
International Bible Society. Used by permission of Zondervan
and Hodder & Stoughton Limited. All rights reserved. The 'NIV'
and 'New International Version' trademarks are registered in the
United States Patent and Trademark Office by International Bible
Society. Use of either trademark requires the permission of
International Bible Society. UK trademark number 1448790.

This book has been printed on paper and board independently
certified as having been produced from sustainable forests

A catalogue record for this book is available
from the British Library

Typeset in 10/12 Berkeley OldStyle
Printed and bound in Wales
by Creative Print and Design

I dedicate this book to my darling children and grandchildren, who mean so much to me. I would not have been able to write the book without them. To my son Ben and his wife Helen, and Hannah and Jessica; my daughter Sarah and her husband Reuben, and Zack, Bethany and Joshua; and my daughter Jayne: thank you for all your encouragement to me to press on and write another book. I hope that you enjoy this one too, and that you are able to pass it on to future generations in our family.

Acknowledgments

I am indebted to Dr Hazel Curtis, Consultant Paediatrician at the Royal Devon and Exeter NHS Foundation Trust, for her very helpful input, her thoughtful suggestions, and the time she gave to reading the manuscript and writing the Foreword. My thanks also go to my lovely assistant Naomi; I really couldn't have done this without you. Your computer skills are amazing, and you are so unflappable and great fun to work with. You calmed me down when I felt the deadline was looming and I still had loads to do. You have always been there for me on the end of the phone just when I needed you. Thanks also to all who have looked after my great-niece Anya to enable Naomi to work with me, especially Rosie.

To all the families I've worked for: thank you for having me into your homes and allowing me the privilege of looking after your babies and children. You have given me so much valuable experience and support in writing. Thank you to all of the parents who wrote letters that gave me snippets of wisdom for this book. I would like also to say a big thank you to those parents who have helped me by giving me ideas and inviting me to come back to look after their second, third and fourth babies. This has given me renewed experience in watching toddlers grow and develop in today's world. It is always a joy to live and work in a home where parents have laid down the important foundations in the early months and the children are happy, secure and well behaved because they know where the boundary lines are.

All of my family have given me great support in writing, once again, and I'd particularly like to thank my daughter Sarah for her insight into life as a busy mum; also my sister Heather for inspiring me to write about the place of peace and contemplation in little ones' lives. Thank you to all at Lion Hudson for encouraging me to write another book and for your help and support throughout. It's been a pleasure to work with Morag Reeve on both books, and I shall miss you as you move to pastures new.

Last but not least, my dear husband John: I couldn't have written this book without your support. Thank you, darling, for all your patience with me as I've spent hours in front of my computer, and sometimes forgotten you were around. Thank you too for keeping the house and garden up and running, and for all your practical help. You've encouraged me again to keep on going.

Contents

Foreword

Rachel's book tackles the complexity and challenge of bringing up toddlers in the twenty-first century. It will help you to understand and nurture your child's physical, emotional and spiritual development. However, it also considers the needs of parents, seeking to help you to juggle the demands and pressures of our frenetic culture, while still enjoying being the mum or dad of a lively toddler. The book is written with a real warmth and an encouraging, practical style, drawing upon Rachel's wealth of experience, gained over many years as a nursery nurse, mother and grandmother and now as a consultant working one-to-one with families.

This book is a treasure trove of information, addressing all aspects of child care and development, including the common problem areas, such as behaviour, sleep and feeding. It offers practical ideas and strategies for handling difficult issues, such as ten top tips for sleeping, and the importance of family mealtimes. The controversial issues are discussed thoughtfully, including the importance of disciplining in a loving, nurturing and consistent way, so that the toddler will be more ready to cope with the wider world of nursery, school and beyond.

I was delighted to see lots of information on play and the top ten toys for the toddler years (DVDs don't make it into the top ten!). Play is an important part of parenting and helps to lay the foundations for so many aspects of development – including language, social skills, creativity and imagination. It is all too easy to be busy, yet play is an important opportunity to just enjoy being together and having fun!

Another valuable part of this book is its emphasis upon nurturing the emotional and spiritual sides of your toddler as well as his or her physical needs. Children thrive on knowing how precious they are and that they are deeply and unconditionally loved. Young children may not fully understand when we say 'I love you', but actions so often speak louder than words.

Rachel acknowledges that there are times when we don't get it right and feel that we are failures, but she also offers hope, reminding us that there is always the chance to start again the next day. Her book will help you to look at the many facets of parenthood, providing inspiration in the midst of the challenges of life with your toddler, whose independence is emerging.

Hazel Curtis
Consultant Paediatrician, Royal Devon and Exeter NHS Foundation Trust
Lead Clinician for Honeylands Child Development Centre

CHAPTER 1

Introduction

Aims of This Book

When my publishers suggested I write another book, I wondered how different it might be from *The Baby Book*. As I have spent time thinking through what parents want to know when bringing up their children, I feel that parenting during the toddler years can be just as much a minefield as caring for a newborn baby.

During the first year of our baby's life we will probably have had all sorts of ups and downs and coped pretty well, and we may think it is easy from now onwards. Once we pass into the second year of our child's life, we may feel we have got it all worked out, and then friends say 'Just wait and see, the terrible twos!' Some parents have seen such awful behaviour in their friends' children that they dread the toddler years, but it doesn't need to be like that. In my experience each stage is precious and exciting as our children do new things, and despite the challenges of the toddler years they also seem to pass very quickly, especially when we look back.

I feel passionate about family life and enjoying our children and I do hope that this book will be a help to you in every way, particularly enabling you to enjoy the toddler years. We will be looking together at the practical aspects of parenting: helping your child to sleep well and eat well, potty training and general care. We will also look at the emotional and spiritual side of our child as he is growing up, and how we can show him love and care to help him to develop into a well-rounded child. I think this part of parenting is very important, particularly in today's world, where everyone is in such a hurry and nobody has any time. Often a child's physical needs are met but not his emotional ones.

I am a great believer in consistent and loving but firm discipline and I know that it is important to lay down good foundations and boundaries in the early years. Parenting in this way will help your toddler to grow up feeling loved and secure. In my view it is vital that our children feel wanted and affirmed. It is also important that our children have a strong sense of belonging and being part of a family, and of knowing that they are loved and cared for. When we show our children love we are teaching them to love others, and this foundation of love needs to be laid down in the early months and years of their life. We need to be open with our children, particularly as they get older and have a deeper understanding and awareness of what is going on around them. All these things will enable them to mature emotionally. One of my good friends has written about the importance of building good memories that children are able to draw on during difficult times of life. I have expanded on these themes in Chapter 13 (Your Toddler's Spiritual and Emotional Needs).

I feel we should remember as parents that little girls are very different from little boys, whatever we may be told, and our approach may be slightly different in the way we parent them. You don't have to spend very long with young children to see how obvious this difference is. Little girls often aspire to being a 'princess', enjoying dressing-up games, playing at mummies and daddies and getting married, whereas many little boys are 'warriors', fight battles, enjoy boisterous play and have an inbuilt desire to provide and protect. In this book I hope to help you as parents to nurture these differences but also to enable your children to socialize and play well with children of both genders.

I always say that we don't get a trial run at parenting. We must do what we feel is right at the time and try not to look back and feel guilty over the mistakes that we are bound to make. There is no such thing as the perfect parent, so if you are struggling, take heart. Most other parents struggle too from time to time. Children are pretty tough and it is amazing how they develop and do well, even if we think we have not done a very good job.

My Background

As the eldest of six children, the youngest of whom is ten years my junior, I grew up in a home where there were always young children around. This is where my love of young children began. My parents had a private maternity nurse for their first four children, and I vividly remember this official-looking woman in a starched uniform coming when my two brothers were born. My father seemed terrified of her, and I certainly was! I remember not being allowed to go into my parents' bedroom to see my mother and the new baby, and feeling very left out. This experience has made me very aware of the importance of including older brothers and sisters in family life when a new baby is born.

At seventeen I attended a Doctor Barnado's residential nursery training college in Kent to train for my National Nursery Examining Board Diploma. My course involved working with many newborn babies and toddlers, which I loved. After completing my training, I went to London for my first job as a maternity nurse, looking after a premature baby. I then moved on to another family with three children under the age of three, where I worked until my marriage. I married a farmer, and we had three children of our own. During those years of bringing up our children, I would help and advise friends with their children. This confirmed my deep feeling that children need a loving routine and structure in their lives from an early age.

After moving to Devon, I returned to work as a nanny helping mums with newborns and young children. I have travelled around the UK and the world with my work over the past decade. Over the years I've had the privilege of going back to families as a maternity nurse for their second or subsequent children.

More recently I have set up a consultancy business in Devon. I offer daily home visits to couples expecting their first baby to prepare them for coming home from hospital with a newborn. We talk through any fears and issues that they may have. I also offer telephone advice to families with new babies and young children who are having sleeping or feeding problems.

I now have five grandchildren, and helping them has been a real joy to me; there's nothing quite like working with your own family.

CHAPTER 2

Bringing Up Children in the Twenty-first Century

Just before I came to write this chapter, UNICEF, the United Nations Children's Fund, published a report entitled *An Overview of Child Well-being in Rich Countries*, of which Britain is one. The report came up with some pretty serious findings. Children in Britain were found to be the unhappiest and loneliest in the developed world. British children were also less fulfilled than any other children in the developed world and had more behavioural problems and a sense of 'not belonging'. So many families today have almost everything that money can buy and yet children still don't feel loved. These statistics make me very sad and they have caused me to think deeply about where we are going wrong in bringing up our children today. I feel that there has been a general breakdown in family life over the past thirty years, and this has fuelled a deep unhappiness in a lot of our children and young people. This has made me realize again the importance of positive, loving, secure parenting.

As I've been writing my books and talking to family members from three generations, a number of themes have emerged which suggest that many people see that positive parenting and family life have been eroded. In this chapter, I hope to set the scene for the rest of the book by talking about some of the changes in parenting and family life that have taken place in society in recent years.

Changes in Society

Fearfulness of Discipline and Boundaries

Sadly, discipline has become an increasingly dirty word in parenting. Let's take a look at its definition in the Oxford English Dictionary: 'Training that produces orderliness, obedience and self-control'. I feel that most parents would agree that these are good things and qualities we would hope for in our children. However, many parents have been afraid of becoming a 'disciplinarian': someone who enforces rules with punishment and imposes rigid discipline. This is particularly true of parents who have had a very strict and rigid upbringing and want to ensure their child does not have the same.

From the 1960s onwards there was a swing in society away from discipline and boundaries for children. In many ways, we may be seeing two generations of children who have been brought up with little clear guidance about what is acceptable behaviour. I think this is one of the reasons there are so many alarming newspaper articles about teenagers' behaviour, television programmes sending the 'experts' in to help families in crisis over 'tearaway toddlers' and reports from teachers of uncontrollable children. I don't believe we should lay the blame upon parents for these changes in society, as many parents were brought up with few boundaries themselves and have been left with a legacy of uncertainty about how best to discipline their own children. But I believe the tide is turning and more and more parents are beginning to realize that having boundaries makes for happier family life.

Children are not born with a set of rules, although at times you may feel they are – usually different from your own! I always say when I am talking to parents that it is *you* who need to set the boundaries. I believe passionately in loving, affirming discipline, which all children need for their all-round development. My aim in this book is to help you to feel confident with your child, to enable you to understand how to lovingly discipline her and to help to put the responsibility of consistent parenting back into your hands. I hope to equip you with methods of positive parenting for the most common problem areas with toddlers: behaviour (Chapter 3), sleep (Chapter 4) and eating (Chapter 5).

Breakdown of Family Relationships

Sadly, there are many reasons why family breakdown occurs. One of the most common is financial pressure, such as worry over unemployment, debt and how to provide for a family. This can lead to arguments between parents, and children soon pick up on the tension in the family, even if they are still very young. Financial pressure can often lead to a burden of overwork for one or both parents. Parents may be working long hours each day and hardly see their children. This can make parents feel guilty, as many would love to spend more time with their children, but the 'busyness' of life just takes over. This sort of existence puts a huge strain on family relationships.

Many parents are continually tired, often due to a heavy workload and the fact that young children can be exhausting. However, this becomes much worse if you're also having broken nights with children who don't sleep well and are up and down all night. Sleep deprivation is most destructive, as you are always just too tired to talk things through. Lack of communication can happen easily, and very soon you feel you're not discussing anything that really matters. When you don't have time or energy to talk, lack of agreement between you as parents – especially on the emotive issues of parenting such as discipline or eating – can lead to problems within the family.

During the 1960s a new divorce law came in which made it much easier for people to get a divorce, and in time there was less stigma around divorce until now nearly half of all marriages in Britain end in divorce. I speak from experience, having gone through divorce myself, and I know the pain it brings not only to the couple but also to the children, whatever their ages. Many couples feel strongly about their marriage vows and believe that marriage is for life, so it is devastating when their marriage ends in the divorce courts. I felt like this and struggled to come to terms with being a single mum, even though my children were older and not all living at home. In my case my husband and I remarried and it has been wonderful to see the healing within our family as well as the wider family. However, I recognize that some marriages are deeply destructive both to parents and children, and divorce is the only way through.

I believe that children need both male and female role models in their lives as they are growing up. Our family relationships act as a role model for our children of how to manage their relationships in adult life. The key ingredients, I believe, are love and stability, giving our children quality time and being consistent. Also, a real sense of fun is important for family life so that we are able to laugh at our mistakes and laugh with our children too. These attributes apply just as much to single-parent families, step-families and parents who only see their children at weekends as to the 'traditional' nuclear family.

Being a mother and a granny, and having worked with numerous families over the years, I understand that family relationships are not always easy. Life is often not straightforward, and just as you think you have everything sorted out, something else happens and you feel you are back to square one. In Chapter 12 I will be giving some practical advice on how to build a strong, secure family life and suggesting ways to help you enjoy being a parent. I will also be talking about how we can show love to our children in Chapter 13, which focuses on the spiritual and emotional needs of your toddler.

Rising Consumerism

I believe our consumer culture puts huge pressure on families. We live in a society in which we often expect to have everything we want materially, and to have it instantly. For some parents there is also a perceived pressure to 'keep up with the Joneses'. This sort of lifestyle can cause tensions in a relationship, and often both parents have to work to service debts or large mortgages.

Many of today's parents were brought up in a relatively affluent society, in which toys and holidays didn't need to be saved up for. Often their expectations for their own children's standard of living are the same or higher. It can be hard to say 'no' to your children when their friends seem to have all the latest gadgets, toys and clothes. Sadly, many parents see gift-giving as the way to show love to their child, especially when parental relationships have broken down. You may be surprised to find how happy young children are with very simple things to play with, rather than expensive presents. What our children crave most of all is our time and love. Loving your child unconditionally and giving him time are the greatest gifts you can ever give him.

I do see positive signs of the pendulum swinging back, with some parents keen to have a 'simpler' childhood for their children and becoming more concerned about consumerism and its impact on the rest of the world. In Chapter 12 on family life, I hope to give you some practical tips on having great times together without spending a lot of money.

Pressures on Parents Today

Living Away from Extended Family

Many people live far away from their extended families today for all sorts of reasons, whereas fifty years ago most couples started married life near their parents. This means that when couples have babies and raise a family they don't have the hands-on help and advice from wider family living nearby. So we don't have a culture of know-how being handed down through the family, and many parents feel isolated. It may be difficult for you to call on grandparents to come in and help or babysit if they are living on the other side of the country or even abroad. The positive side of this is that friendships become very important to families. I believe strong and lasting friendships are built as you share with friends the ups and downs of having babies and bringing up young children.

Different Family Structures

Children are brought up in many different family settings today. Step-families often have their problems as parents try to bring children together in a family unit. This can often be difficult, especially for toddlers who may become unsettled in new surroundings and confused as they miss the other parent. There are many more single parents now and often these are mums, struggling to bring up children on their own in very tough circumstances. This can be because of separation, divorce or bereavement, and parenting can feel very lonely in these circumstances. In some families one parent will often only see the children at weekends and in the holidays. This is also difficult, often for both parties. It is important for parents to try to be civil to each other and not attempt to score off one another, and to try to put the children's needs before their own. This can be particularly hard to do, especially when one party has walked out. Children suffer just as much as parents do through separation and divorce. Try to remember that it isn't your child's fault that you separated, as she can soon feel it was if you load on her your feelings of anguish. If you are struggling with any of these issues, try to get help and mediation.

Working Life for Parents

There has been an apparent culture shift towards a 'work-life balance', which I think is very welcome, but I am not sure that some companies are really that good on flexible working yet; there is still room for improvement! It is more accepted that women will work part-time, but in general it seems to be difficult for men to have this flexibility too. Many fathers work away from home all week and come home at weekends feeling absolutely shattered. This sort of lifestyle is becoming more common and can put pressure on a relationship, especially for the mother, who has been looking after the children on her own all week. It can be hard on dads too, as they come back into the family for short periods and then have to go away again. Many fathers work long hours, going off to work before the children are up in the mornings and coming back long after they are in bed. Long working hours are difficult to live with but the reality is that many have them, and the important thing to remember is to talk together about how you are both coping and to build time in for each other. If possible make weekends and holidays special family times, and remember that it does get easier as the children get older.

A Culture of Busyness

There is a danger, I think, of children's lives being too busy and over-structured. There are so many activities on offer, from dancing classes to music to gym, and of course the endless round of play dates to be fitted into the social diary. These can be an added strain on family life, particularly if you have several children and are rushing round in circles trying to get them to their clubs and societies. This can hugely escalate with after-school activities, and it is becoming increasingly the case for toddlers too. Try to remember that children need time just to *be* and are often just as happy being at home with you, playing with their toys and spending time with you in an unhurried way.

Too Many Expert Opinions

Many parents say to me that they are given too many 'expert opinions', starting from the moment of conception! Mums especially can be overwhelmed with numerous instructions, such as what they should and shouldn't eat, what type of exercise they should take, what they must buy for the nursery and so on. As I talk to parents I find a real sense of fear about what they should be doing with their child, whether it involves feeding, sleeping or potty training. Parents say that the advice keeps changing; in fact each time they have a baby the advice is different from before! There are huge concerns over food allergies today, for example, and I worry that these can be taken so far that we move away from a sensible and balanced approach to feeding our children.

Positive Changes for Parents Today

I seem to have talked a lot about negatives in the above paragraphs, and now I want to concentrate on the positive changes that are happening for parents today. Sometimes I wish I could start all over again and have my family for a second time when I see the opportunities that young families have nowadays.

Extended Family through Friendships

The way that friends support each other in the absence of the wider family is lovely to see. There has been a huge growth in National Childbirth Trust (NCT), toddler and preschool groups over the last few years. These all help new parents to get to know others with young babies and children and provide a place where you can share experiences, tips and problems. It is encouraging to know that you are not alone and that you are all going through similar experiences. Often at these groups someone who has had lots of experience with young children will visit and give advice too. Some of the friendships you make through these groups are long-lasting, as they form at a very special time in your life. There is also good Internet support for mums through websites such as Mumsnet (www.mumsnet.com) and chat rooms, helping you to know you are not on your own.

Involvement of Family, Especially Grandparents, in Childcare

When families do live near grandparents or other relatives, it is much more common nowadays for them to be involved in childcare and supporting parents in bringing up children. In fact, today you see more and more grandparents at the school gates collecting children from school. Some parents actually pay family members to help with childcare, and this can work very well, especially if relatives are on a low income and the parents are earning good wages. Close relatives can be a great asset to families, as they are familiar to the children and have a unique relationship with them. Being a grandparent, an uncle or an aunt is a very special role and it is a real privilege to be involved with the children, whether in day-to-day childcare or on special visits and family gatherings.

Greater Recognition of the Importance of Fathers

Another good thing that has happened in society is the way that dads are encouraged to be much more involved in their child's life right from birth. It is a contrast with the post-war generation, when child-rearing was quite exclusively female and fathers often didn't get a look in. When our eldest child was born in the early 1970s my husband was allowed to be with me for his birth, but that was quite unusual. Nowadays almost all fathers are present for the birth of their child, are actively involved in supporting their partner in labour and are encouraged to be involved in babycare from the start. I think it is very special to see dads doing these practical things for their babies. The toddler years can be a great time for deeper bonding between fathers and children, especially if the child has been exclusively breastfed for the first year of his life. Employers are beginning to recognize the need for family time for fathers, but as I have already said, there is definitely room for improvement. Finally, research on children's educational attainment and emotional health has led to an increasing recognition of the vital importance of the role of dads in children's lives.

Greater Choice Over Working Life

Parents nowadays have many more options over their working life. It is much more acceptable today for the father to stay at home and look after a child while the mother goes back to work, and for some families this works very well. Some parents are able to share, with both working part-time, so that one of them is at home doing childcare while the other is at work. However, the decision about who goes back to work and when can be quite a challenge, particularly with a second child. Childcare is not always easy to decide on and needs to make sense financially. Your child can go to a nursery or a childminder; you could employ a nanny, or use grandparents if they live nearby. All of these options need to be looked at thoroughly before choosing the option that suits your child and your budget.

I firmly believe that parents should be encouraged and given all the help they need to build up their confidence in parenting. In fact, I think all parents should have the opportunity to take part in parenting classes if they wish to as they are bringing up their children. The UK charity Care for the Family have developed an excellent course called Parentalk, which is delivered across the country (www.parentalk.co.uk).

Closing Thoughts

While researching this book, I wrote to a number of my friends and clients who've been through the toddler years. I asked them to tell me what they wished they had known before entering the toddler years, and I feel these responses speak volumes:

'To trust my own instincts more, and relax and enjoy.'

'Things get easier, and time passes far too fast (in hindsight).'

'Treasure all that is so precious about a marvellous (and slightly mad) journey.'

'Keep a sense of humour and don't worry about the sticky fingers.'

When I talk to groups of parents I always affirm them in what they are doing. Parenting is one of the most valuable jobs you will ever do in your lifetime, as you are building the next generation, and that in itself is priceless. Please don't underestimate the importance of the job you are doing, even if you feel you are not doing it properly. There is no such thing as the perfect parent, and none of us gets a trial run at it. My hope is that this book will be a guide, an inspiration and a comfort to you as you read it. I hope that you will benefit from the experience I have had with families and young children over the years and develop your own confidence as a parent.

CHAPTER 3

Your Toddler's Behaviour

Often when we talk to friends about having a toddler, they make a face and say, 'Oh, how are you getting on – have you got to the terrible twos yet?' I honestly think that parenting toddlers can be almost as exhausting as parenting teenagers. Yet the joys of having little ones can quite override those times when we feel we have said 'no' all day. When we think and talk of the toddler years we so often think of tantrums, yet the reality is that for a large proportion of the time they're a great source of joy. Toddlers have a tremendous sense of fun and are open and communicative with all those around them. They giggle and laugh at new things and little games, it doesn't take much to please them, they don't hold grudges, and they will smile and play even if you have been telling them off. They seem to be endlessly cheeky in a lovely sort of way, they have lots of energy and always want to play and explore the world around them. They can be a delight, particularly to grandparents and relatives, who can hand them back at the end of the day when your energy levels are nil!

However, the flip-side is that toddlers are growing and becoming more independent, and part of their exploration is the need to test boundaries. At some point, all toddlers will get frustrated as they can't do what they want to do, and this will lead to sudden outbursts of emotion. One minute they are happily playing, and the next minute they will be wailing at some small setback that seems a catastrophe to them. Toddlers can also seem very negative as they begin to assert their independence; some days it will seem as though all they say is 'no, no, no'. Toddlers aren't born with a code of behaviour, and in these early years children watch how you respond to their different actions. This is why being consistent about boundaries is so important, as toddlers are forming a system of rules about life in their minds and need to know from you what the rules are. Children understand a great deal even if they are not yet talking, so it's never too early to start laying boundaries down.

In this chapter, I hope to give you an overview of what good behaviour looks like in toddlers and why it's so important to give your child boundaries early in life. The main focus of the chapter, however, will be the types of difficult behaviour you are likely to encounter during the toddler years, as undoubtedly you will. My aim is to give you a range of practical methods for dealing with this behaviour, using methods whereby 'no' is kept to a minimum. I can only give you a guide to the methods that have worked well for myself and others; I hope you'll be able to pick and choose from these to find what suits you and your child best.

Establishing Good Behaviour

What is Good Behaviour?

The understanding of what is 'good behaviour' is different for different people. Some parents have a very high standard of behaviour and will not tolerate unruliness, whereas other parents are more laid-back about how their children behave. Personally I believe that good behaviour is when a child responds when told what to do by an adult, whether at home or out and about. I know that this doesn't always happen, as children have their ups and downs, but in general a child who has been taught this expectation of good behaviour will usually respond well to an adult's wishes.

I believe there are universal codes of behaviour that apply to everyone, for example, not causing harm to others, respecting people and property, and having control over one's emotions. These are the things that we need to teach our children so that they can grow up to be responsible and law-abiding adults. Intervening to stop your child from lashing out at other children or adults is vital in teaching her that this is unacceptable behaviour. Teaching your child not to scribble on walls, stand or jump on furniture or throw food around is all part of establishing good, responsible behaviour.

Politeness, especially saying 'please' and 'thank you', is another part of society's expectations of good behaviour. You can teach this to your child, first by using 'please' and 'thank you' when you speak to him and to others, and then by encouraging (not nagging) him to use these words when he asks for things. This is the beginning of teaching your child patience, as you help him to understand that you won't respond to an instant demand such as 'more!' without him first saying 'please'. Teaching such behaviour enables your child to get on with other people and to have respect for them. We all want our children to grow up and be able to have good relationships in life and if they have been disciplined in a loving, consistent way they will be able to do this.

Why Should We Teach Good Behaviour?

Why do we want our children to behave? First, it's going to make it much easier for us as parents and as a family unit. Secondly, our children will be able to mix well with other friends and adults if they know how to behave well and know the difference between right and wrong. Thirdly, it will make their life easier once they go to nursery or school, where a certain code of behaviour will be expected. Finally, we want them to grow and mature into responsible adults who can hold their own in society.

It is important to teach your child what is acceptable and what is unacceptable behaviour from an early age. This will safeguard her from dangers, help her to learn self-control and increase her emotional stability. Having a well-behaved child helps to protect your sanity as parents and gives you space to enjoy your child. Teaching your child what behaviour you expect of her helps you all to be more relaxed when you go out or visit other people. On the whole, children who have clear boundaries for their behaviour are happy and settled – most of the time! However, some children find it much more difficult to conform, and despite your best efforts you may feel you're not making any headway. In this case, I can't overemphasize the importance of persevering and being as consistent as you can with your expectations and boundaries. All children need limits and boundaries and thrive on them, and as parents you have to be the ones to decide what the boundaries are.

What Happens When We Don't Teach Good Behaviour?

If we're honest, as parents we all tell our children off at some point, whether we believe in discipline or not. Often the problems happen when we are inconsistent, so that we tell our child off for something on one occasion and ignore it or laugh at it on another. This is easy to do, especially when we're tired and it's the end of the day, and I've certainly been guilty of this as a mum. However, regular inconsistency over behaviour can bewilder a child, and very soon he will be completely muddled about what is acceptable or unacceptable behaviour. This can make him feel very insecure and he will be more likely to behave badly, almost as if to test out the limits.

A consistent lack of boundaries and discipline can make it difficult for a child to mix with other children, as she won't know how to behave. Often other children won't want to play with her as she will be unpredictable, and she can become isolated. This can be a real problem at nursery or school, particularly if she is disruptive and has to be removed from other children. A child who hasn't learned to respond well to adult direction will often find it hard to listen and conform, and if she's being told off regularly at nursery or school this can make her feel negative. Equally, at home a child may be constantly cross if she doesn't understand why she's being reprimanded, and this can knock her self-esteem. As she gets older, a child who has not been given consistent boundaries will often get into trouble wherever she goes, and may have very little idea how to control her emotions. She will most likely have a very short fuse, particularly when reprimanded about her behaviour. Many children who've grown up without clear guidance about their behaviour are unhappy and insecure.

Difficult Toddler Behaviour

As you enter the toddler years you will notice that your child becomes much more vocal and demanding, as well as more active and mobile. You may have had a very placid baby and it can seem that your child is now growing into a little monster! He may shout, seem to cry more and always want his own way. If your child is anything like this, don't despair, as it is perfectly normal. Remember that your child does need to do some things wrong to learn about boundaries, and he will push those boundaries – it is all part of his development. As the mother of three grown-up children, I can promise you that this will pass and your child will be lovely again. Below are some of the most common toddler behaviours that parents find challenging. If you're in the thick of toddler tantrums at the moment, you may wish to skip straight to the section on ways of managing behaviour (pp. 34–40).

Crying and Anxiety

Why do toddlers seem to cry so much? Most toddlers will cry when they are frightened or unsure of what is happening. This will often be when you take her somewhere new, or maybe when you first leave her at nursery and she is worried because you are going away. She is very likely to cling to your legs and bury her head in them and be quite upset about you going. Many toddlers can become nervous and will cry at sudden noises or unexpected things, such as animals or people in costumes. This is the time for gentle reassurance, cuddles and taking time to settle her in to the new situation.

Most toddlers will cry and be very miserable when they are tired, and this often happens when they've rushed around and worn themselves out. You may find that you get home from a fun morning at a toddler group and suddenly your child is in pieces. Often the best thing to do is to give him a quiet story and a nap, and everything will be much better when he wakes up. Your toddler will also often cry in frustration, particularly when you take something away that he wants or when a toy doesn't work the way he wants it to. This is all part of learning that things don't always go his way.

Demanding Attention

Many toddlers make a huge fuss when you speak to somebody on the telephone and this can be very annoying, especially if it is a business call. You may often find that your child will start whingeing or doing something naughty as soon as she sees you pick up the phone or someone calls you. She may also get cross when you are doing the housework or standing chatting to other parents at the shops or at the school gate. All of this behaviour is down to the fact that she wants your attention and doesn't want you to be giving it to somebody else. When this happens, it's important to tell her that you're talking and she will have to wait a little while. This helps her to gradually learn about being patient, although this will take time and she will need to be reminded; patience is not a toddler virtue!

Toddlers can get bored easily and then will often start to play up. Make sure that there is plenty for him to do and that you don't just leave him to get on by himself for too long. Of course he must learn to play by himself, but if he spends too long without different things to do this can lead to bad behaviour. A toddler's concentration span is very short. Try to be one step ahead of your child so that you can see if he's getting bored. Being quick to suggest a new game or activity is often the essence. However, you mustn't feel that you have to provide a constant stream of entertainment for your child. If you are busy doing the housework, your toddler can either 'help out' with a duster or find something to do while he waits for you to finish.

Wanting Independence

You will find that as your toddler becomes more independent she will want to put her own coat or shoes on, often just as you are rushing to get out. If you can, start getting ready to go out in plenty of time so that you can make a game of putting her coat on. Sometimes having a race with your child will encourage her to get her coat or shoes on, saying 'Who's going to be ready first?' Children love games, and this sort of thing often works. However, if you're having a struggle and if the weather is not really cold or wet, then let her go without a coat but take it with you. This applies to hats and gloves too. Some things are not important enough to have a battle over.

Another common struggle is when you need to put your child in his buggy and he wants to walk. He may go quite stiff and throw himself about to try to stop you from putting him in the buggy. This can also happen with a car seat. You need to be strong and determined that he is going in, and just lift him up and strap him in with no debate. This can feel stressful and embarrassing if you're in public, but you will usually find that once he is strapped in he will calm down again and all will be well.

Toddlers often get frustrated when they try to do things independently that they're just not big enough to do yet: get into their own highchair, do a puzzle or shape-sorter that is too difficult, or pour milk onto their own cereal. None of these in themselves is wrong, but you'll often have to take away the toy or stop your child doing something, simply because she's not ready to do it yet and will get cross if you try to help. Keep giving your child opportunities to try things that are a bit tricky, as in time she will be able to do them. Use your judgement about the things that she's not ready for yet.

Being Self-willed

During the toddler years, you'll probably find that your child will become more self-willed and want to make his own choices. You will also notice that he often says 'no, no, no' when he wants to have his own way, and may say 'no' to every choice you offer him. This is normal behaviour, showing that your child wants to assert his growing independence, but in reality he's not yet ready to make sensible decisions all the time. As parents, it's right for you to make choices and decisions for your toddler even if he protests. Remember, you are the adult, so you don't have to automatically give in to your toddler's demands or refusals. Having said that, toddlers love to have some choices, as it makes them feel very grown-up. You can try giving them 'either-or' options such as 'Would you like ham or cheese?' or 'Shall we play with the ball or the cars?' to avoid the endless word 'no'.

Jealousy When a New Baby Arrives

You may find that even a well-behaved toddler turns into a little horror when you have a new baby, and you wonder what you have in your midst. You may find that she is fine for the first few weeks and then her behaviour changes. She may be unsettled, waking at night, not eating and being very crotchety. She may even hit out at you, especially when you are feeding the baby. She may throw herself on the floor and kick and scream and throw her toys around the room. She is likely to take it out on Mum more than Dad, as Mum is probably the one who does most of the babycare, especially if you are breast-feeding. Make sure that your child doesn't lash out at the baby when she is behaving like this. These are all signs of jealousy, as she wants your full attention and will take time to get used to another little person in the house. You need to give her lots of love and attention when you can so that she doesn't feel left out. You may find that your toddler loves her sibling at first, until the baby starts growing up and taking more of your attention. Again this is jealousy, which needs to be handled with love and care. I have written in detail about this in Chapter 11, on having another baby.

Physical Tantrums

At some point, almost all toddlers will throw themselves on the floor and show real physical rage. Many children scream or bang their heads on the floor during a tantrum, and they will often look round to see how you react. Some children are more prone to tantrums and have them quite regularly through the toddler years, whereas others may be much more placid. Tantrums often happen out of sheer frustration, as toddlers find it hard to cope when they can't do something they are trying to learn to do. The other big flash point for tantrums is when your child does not want to do something that you have asked him to do, and often this happens when you are out and about. Tantrums can be scary for you as a parent, but they can also be quite frightening for your child as he loses control. The main thing is for you to keep as calm and reassuring as you possibly can.

Calmly ignoring a tantrum and waiting for it to pass works well in general. However, the time to intervene with a tantrum is when your child is in danger of hurting herself, for example banging her head on a hard floor, or if she is lashing out at you or another child. Either way, your child will probably need lots of hugs and reassurance once the tantrum is over. This helps her to feel that you have resolved things and that it's all right to express difficult emotions like frustration. I have written in more depth about managing tantrums later on in this chapter (p. 39–40).

Unsafe or Destructive Behaviour

There are things that are simply not safe for your child to do, and as a parent you will need to intervene, even though he will almost certainly protest. Your child needs to know that it is not acceptable to poke his fingers into electrical sockets, pull electrical flexes, run out into the road or climb onto furniture that he could easily fall off and hurt himself. Toddlers are explorers by nature, and unfortunately these things will hold great appeal; but it's important to clearly teach these boundaries to your child so that he learns to play safely as he grows up.

Most toddlers will be quite destructive at times, for example, tearing up books, breaking or throwing toys and drawing on the walls or furniture. Some toddlers will pick things up around the house and hurl them hard, sometimes breaking or damaging them. It's easy to feel that your child is doing this just to be horrible; however, unless you tell her, she has no idea that this is any more naughty than her normal play. The key thing is to deal with this behaviour quickly so that your toddler understands that it is just not acceptable to do these things. Any behaviour that hurts others, such as biting, spitting, kicking or hitting, must be dealt with swiftly by removing your child from the situation and telling her in a very definite, strong voice that she must not behave this way.

Ways of Managing Behaviour

Families vary enormously and there are lots of different approaches to discipline. One of the most important things is to agree with your partner where you are going to set the boundaries of what is acceptable behaviour and what to do when your child breaks these boundaries. If you don't agree, as your child gets older he will pick up that you are divided on this and will very likely play one of you off against the other. I think it is also important for you as parents not to have disagreements about discipline in front of your child. This will be a learning process for you as you go along and you may think that you have no experience with toddlers and don't know what to do. Or you may be keen to discipline your children in a way that differs from your own experience of growing up. I hope in this section to give you practical guidance on many different methods you can choose from.

I don't believe we should go back to forms of discipline that are so rigid that we have unhappy children, such as those that were used in Victorian times, when children were meant to 'be seen and not heard'. Thankfully, we have come a long way from that; but sadly we seem to have gone in the other direction and often there is no place in the family for discipline at all. Over-indulging your child and being very easy on discipline can be as damaging as being totally rigid, and I advise parents to try to find a middle road that suits them.

Love and Consistency

The two main things that will help you to best discipline your child, whatever age she is, are love and consistency. It is important to love your child whatever stage of behaviour she is going through, even when you may not always feel like it. Never withhold affection from your child as a means of discipline. When you have had to tell her off or punish her, spend time afterwards making sure that she understands why you did this and that you love her very much; it was her behaviour that you didn't like. It can be helpful to 'close' tantrums like this, and it helps your child to feel forgiven and move on to the next thing.

It is also important to be consistent in disciplining our children, as far as we possibly can. This means that we build up trust with our child and he knows he can rely on us. Even when children are too young to fully understand, that bond of trust is developed when we are consistent and we do what we say. If you feel strongly about a certain behaviour, it's important to be firm and consistent about the method of discipline you use to deal with it. However, you need flexibility for things that maybe aren't as serious, and for the times when you know that your child is ill or tired and this is affecting his behaviour. Always remember, too, that when *you* are tired it is more difficult to make a sound judgement, and you may need a few seconds to cool down before you decide what to do. Keep the lines of communication open with your child, so that you give him clear warnings about his behaviour and the consequences if he continues. Children change as they grow up and the behaviour patterns you see when they are little may be different as they get older, so you need to talk to both your partner and your child about how the boundaries and discipline will change in order to keep up.

Positive Attention

'Praise, praise, praise' is a very good method of managing your child's behaviour. Your child will learn a lot about good behaviour if you give far more attention to the things you like her doing than to the things you don't. Always praise her for the good things she does so that she hears more positives in a day than negatives. Children seem to thrive on encouragement and being affirmed.

Giving your child lots of love, affection, touch and cuddles is important too. It's much easier to do this when your child is playing happily and bringing stories for you to read, but it's also vital when he's crabby, tired and difficult. Children also thrive on being cuddled and knowing that they can come to you for this affection when they need to. Often, children will need a hug and some reassurance after they know they've behaved badly, and this can help you both to put it behind you.

On the flip-side, negative attention and negative comments about your child can actually reinforce difficult behaviour. One of the main needs that toddlers have is to be noticed and given attention, especially by their parents, and if you only take notice when she's being naughty, she may settle for that. The antidote is to spend small amounts of time giving your child undivided attention, such as playing with her teddies or reading a book, and then teaching her to wait for a little while when you need to have your attention elsewhere. If you can, try to avoid telling your child how bad or naughty she is, and don't talk about her bad behaviour or make negative remarks about her in front of other adults.

Ignoring Bad Behaviour

If your child is behaving badly or having a tantrum you can choose to ignore it. Often, this stops the difficult behaviour in its tracks, as you are not giving your child what he wants – your attention. I have found time and time again that to ignore bad behaviour, if it is not too serious, works well. If your child is safe then walk away from where he is, don't give him eye contact and pretend you haven't noticed what he is doing.

I always use this technique first if what a child is doing is not life-threatening. You will find that she is likely to stop what she is doing and look at you, and if she realizes you are not interested and are walking away, she will probably come and find you. Also, walking out of the situation gives you a breathing space and allows you to collect your thoughts. One of my clients told me that they have a 'lie-down' technique when their child has a tantrum and throws herself on the floor. They say to her, 'You stay there and have a lie down now', and leave her to get over it. These parents say it usually works very quickly, and their child gets up as soon as she realizes nobody is taking any notice.

Distraction

Distraction often works well, and is similar to ignoring the situation. This method focuses on doing something positive instead of engaging in a battle with your child. Distraction seems to work particularly well when children are young. When dealing with tantrums in the early toddler years, I would always try distraction first. Although minor upsets can be overcome by ignoring them, sometimes that's not quite enough. This approach works on the basis that the less fuss you make over things, the less often they escalate into a real humdinger.

If your child is having a tantrum and you can 'change the subject', as I call it, this often works brilliantly. If your child is really cross, pick him up, pretending you haven't noticed his temper, take him to the window and ask him what he can see. Make a little story up about what you see out of the window and say that maybe a dog or a car or whatever is just coming. This sort of talk often changes his attitude immediately and you will find that he will stop crying and be happy to go on playing.

Giving your child something to do when she is cross can often take her mind off what is bothering her. This is another form of distraction, and can diffuse a situation before it happens. Often you can see that your child is working up to either throwing something across the room or grabbing a toy from another child. You need to pitch in and distract her with another activity before that happens. Having a sense of humour with your child also helps to lighten things. Sometimes if a child is being grumpy with me I laugh and say, 'What a funny face to make!', maybe making a face like hers, and we will then laugh and it diffuses the situation. Sometimes I will pretend to cry if the child has said something I don't like; again, this often has quite an impact and diffuses the difficult behaviour.

I used this method of distraction recently with one of our grandchildren and it worked immediately. We had had a long car journey through France, followed by a ferry crossing to England. We were all very tired, especially the children. It was time for her to get into the car again, but she didn't want to and went stiff, throwing her arms and legs around. There were a couple of large rocks that she had been jumping on and off into my arms a few minutes before, so I said, 'Let's go and play on the stones once more.' She ran and had a couple of jumps into my arms and then got straight into the car without a fuss. Distraction had worked again and meant that there was no ongoing tantrum.

I have found that singing to babies and young children has a very calming effect. Over the years I have often soothed an upset child by playing the piano and singing; it seems to work wonderfully, especially when they are tired and it is the end of the day. If you have some relaxing music on a CD, or if you play an instrument or like to sing, you could try this. Most children find nursery rhymes distracting and may join in with the actions, so any upset will be forgotten.

Time Out

Sometimes your child will need to be removed from the company of others because his behaviour is not acceptable. Many parents use a 'naughty step' or put their child in another room to cool down. When our children were young we either sat them on the bottom step of the stairs, and they had to stay there and think about what they had done, or they went to their bedroom. This works well for many toddlers, especially children who have the sort of personality that means they don't like to miss out on all that's going on.

To use 'time out', warn your child of what you are going to do, so that you give her the opportunity to behave and to calm down. If you do have to remove your child to a place you have chosen, decide how long you are going to leave her there, and make sure there aren't any toys around that she can play with and so forget why she is there. If she is upset and very sorry for what she has done, leave her for a couple of minutes, then go to her and ask her to say sorry to whoever it is that she has upset. If you removed her because of a tantrum, then ask her to say sorry for having a temper, and explain that you don't like that kind of behaviour. When she does apologize, give her a cuddle and tell her you have forgiven her. When you have resolved what has happened, move on and try not to bring it up again unless she starts behaving in the same way, and then you can warn her about what happened last time. This can help your child to grow up with the ability to resolve issues in adult life.

In some cases, your child's behaviour may be so unacceptable that you need to remove him immediately without a warning. It is perfectly all right to do this. This would include behaviour such as hitting or biting another child or having a completely out-of-control tantrum. As parents, you will have your own boundaries for what behaviour warrants immediate removal. When dealing with this sort of behaviour, always try to keep your voice as calm and level as possible, being firm without shouting. Say very definitely to your child that he must not do that, and that he is going to have some time out because that was very naughty. When my children had behaved extremely badly, they would go to their rooms or into their cot for a little while, as this seemed a more definite removal than just the bottom step. In my experience, this didn't make our children think of their bedrooms as horrible places to be at other times.

If your child refuses to stay where you have decided she must go when she is naughty, the first thing to do is to keep taking her back. She may have to stay there longer if she is not sorry for what she has done. If this doesn't work, then I would suggest using a stairgate so that she cannot get out of the area where you put her, making sure of course that she is safe. Once the 'time out' is over, always talk to your child and explain what she has done, and say that it makes Mummy and Daddy very sad when they see her behaving like this. Always get down on your child's level with her, and put your arm round her so that you are showing that you love her even though she has behaved badly. Remember that the amount of time out will depend on your child's age and her level of understanding.

Managing Physical Tantrums

If your child throws himself on the floor and has a real kicking, flailing tantrum, try not to worry, as this is a perfectly normal part of toddler life. In the first instance, I would let your child know that you don't like this behaviour and that it's really silly, and ask him if he wants to get up and do something with you. However, you will sometimes find that your child is so worked up that he won't be able to do this, and I feel the best thing to do in this case is just to leave him to thrash it out, as long as he is safe. Tell him that you're going out of the room and that he can come and find you when he is feeling better. You need to be somewhere where you can see him through the door and keep an eye on him. You will probably find that when he realizes you are not taking any notice he will stop shouting and get up. He may well come to find you and be upset and sobbing. Get down on his level, put your arms around him and say something like, 'That was silly, Mummy doesn't like all that fuss. Come and say sorry and we will have a cuddle and make it better.' Again, make sure you resolve it, even if your child is just entering the toddler years, as this will help him to move on from tantrums better when he is older.

Many parents ask me how to cope with tantrums when they are out and about, especially when they happen in the supermarket or the street. It is a case of 'needs must' when you are out, so don't feel guilty about buying a treat or some sweets to placate your child. Try distracting your child by looking at things in the shops or making a game out of finding things in the supermarket. If your child has gone past the point of being distracted, then you can either abandon your trip and go home or make the best of it and get home as soon as you can. It is best to avoid punishing your child in front of other people, as it can be embarrassing for you and everyone seems to have an opinion about whether you're doing it right or not. If your child is older, you can tell her that she is going to her room or cannot play with her toy when she gets home because she has misbehaved.

Of course, as your child understands more you can more easily tell him that having physical tantrums is just not acceptable. By the age of three you will find that you can be very definite with him, as he is old enough for you to reason with, and tell him that it is not behaviour that Daddy and Mummy like. Make a point of talking to your child, explaining, 'We don't behave like that in our family.'

Punishment

Although I can give you some guidelines, you as parents both need to be happy with the sort of punishment you are going to use. Ideally this will only need to be used on infrequent occasions, especially if you have set down firm boundaries when your child is young. Sanctions such as taking toys and treats away are a form of punishment in themselves, and I have found that some children respond very well to this and will understand quickly why you have made these sanctions. For example, if your child has just crayoned on the wall, then take her crayons away so that she understands that this behaviour is not acceptable. Make sure the punishment fits the crime, so that really special toys are only taken away after a clear warning and when your child has done something quite unacceptable, such as constantly refusing to share. As your child gets older, taking treats away will mean more to her than to a young toddler. Always warn your child first that that you are going to remove a treat or a toy and then, if her behaviour hasn't improved, do what you have decided to do. It is important not just to threaten the punishment but to carry it out. If you don't your child will not believe you and will not understand the consequences of her bad behaviour.

I believe I should talk about smacking as a form of punishment even though it is a very emotive subject today. There are many parents who feel there are plenty of other ways in which to discipline their children other than smacking. They feel that by using physical punishment they are teaching their child to hit out, and worry that he may smack other children. Some parents feel they could not smack their child whatever the reason, in just the same way they would feel about hitting an adult. These objections to smacking are all very valid and I strongly believe this is a completely personal decision for you as parents to make. You need to talk it through together and you may find that you have differing views, maybe depending on how your own parents disciplined you. It is important that you agree on your method of punishment, as differing views could come between you and cause problems in your relationship and your parenting.

Some parents, however, do smack their children and find it a very effective form of punishment, especially when it is not used often. Parents who use smacking say to me that they often find that simply warning their child that she will be smacked if she continues to misbehave stops the child in her tracks. What I feel I must stress at this point is that hitting out at a child in anger is completely different from a controlled smack after a clear warning. If you are going to use smacking I cannot emphasize enough that it must never be done in anger or as a way of letting off steam at your child, however naughty she has been. Lashing out physically is abusive, just as much as losing your temper completely and shouting and screaming at your child. Likewise, never shake your child. These are all abusive behaviours and are not discipline. All these abusive methods will upset and confuse your child, and could cause her real problems in adult life. If you find yourself in a situation of wanting to lash out at your child in any way, walk away to calm down. You must then get some help, maybe by asking somebody to come in and take over while you take some time to cool down.

Closing Thoughts

My hope is that this chapter has helped you not to feel that dealing with your toddler's behaviour is a minefield. Often as parents we are afraid of setting down boundaries and disciplining our children when necessary. I hope that this chapter has helped to dispel some of that fear and helped you to feel that you have some techniques to choose from in managing your toddler's behaviour at these challenging times – which *will* come! Even if you are parenting second or third time around, it can be surprising how different children respond to different types of behaviour management. What works for one child may not work as well for the next. It's a learning process as your children grow up, but a privilege to see that you have enabled them to develop a sense of right and wrong and to respect boundaries.

Children Learn What They Live

If children live with criticism, they learn to condemn.
If children live with hostility, they learn to fight.
If children live with ridicule, they learn to feel shy.
If children live with shame, they learn to feel guilty.

If children live with encouragement, they learn confidence.
If children live with tolerance, they learn patience.
If children live with praise, they learn appreciation.
If children live with acceptance, they learn to love.

If children live with approval, they learn to like themselves.
If children live with honesty, they learn truthfulness.
If children live with security, they learn to have faith in themselves and in those about them.
If children live with friendliness, they learn the world is a nice place in which to live.

Dorothy Law Nolte

CHAPTER 4

Sleep

As I travel round the country with my work and I meet and talk with different families, I find that children's sleeping habits are a big issue. It is quite natural to be concerned if our children don't sleep well, as we know the effects it has on all the family. I used to say when my children were little, 'If I can get a good night's sleep I can cope with anything in the day!' In my training I learned the value of setting down good sleeping patterns in the early months of a baby's life. As a consequence, our children were all good sleepers; they had to be, as we were busy farmers.

It is important to introduce good sleeping patterns when your child is young. It's much easier to set down a good sleep routine before your child begins to really battle over bedtime. However, don't despair if you have an older toddler who is not sleeping well. It is not too late to do sleep training, although to be honest, it will take longer. In this chapter I am going to talk about how much sleep your toddler needs, how to establish good sleeping habits and how to deal with sleep problems.

If you have read *The Baby Book*, you may be wondering what the routine timings are for your toddler. Between the ages of one and three children's needs for sleep change and vary so much that I would say there is room for a lot of flexibility within your daily routine. In this chapter I've aimed to give you rough timings, suggesting two naps a day for younger toddlers and one nap a day for older toddlers. In fact, you may find that a three-year-old drops daytime sleeps altogether. For an at-a-glance summary I have set out guideline timings for a flexible routine for toddlers aged one, two and three in the Appendix (pp. 187–89).

How Much Sleep Does My Toddler Need?

Many parents ask me how much their young child should be sleeping, and as we know, some children are good sleepers whereas others seem to survive on very little sleep. Up until the age of three, your child will need around 12 to 14 hours of sleep a day. By the time your baby is a year old he should be sleeping well at night, from about 7 p.m. to 7 or 8 a.m. He should also be having one good nap in the day and still having a short nap in the afternoon. He should be easy to settle to sleep, enjoy being in his cot during the day if you are at home, and be happy to be tucked into his cot again in the evening. If you lay down good sleeping habits during the early months of his life, you will find that in general your child is happy to settle on his own and will sleep well.

From about eighteen months you will find that your toddler's daytime sleeping changes, especially if she sleeps well at night. She may only need one good sleep in the day and every now and again will want a short afternoon nap. Be flexible with her as she changes, as some days she may still need two naps. By the time your toddler is about two years old she may only be napping for a short time in the day, and some days may not need a nap at all. Children are all different and some need a daytime nap for longer than others, so if you find that she is grumpy and getting overtired, let her have a nap when she needs to.

Good Sleeping Habits

To encourage good sleep, it is important that your child has enough fresh air and exercise and plenty to eat and drink during the day and doesn't go to bed hungry. It's also important to have regular nap times and a structured bedtime routine. Young children need to be settling down for bed by 7 p.m., and it's worth remembering that putting your child to bed later in the evening does not usually mean that he will sleep until later in the morning. A pattern of late bedtimes will mean that your child easily gets overtired and can be more difficult both during the day and at bedtime. In contrast, a child who sleeps well is a real joy to have around, as he will usually be happy and contented and fun to be with.

Bedtime Routines

It is important to have a good bedtime routine for your toddler, and ideally you will have put this into place in the early months of her life. If not, it is a good idea to start now and not wait any longer. I often say to parents that it's much easier to introduce good sleeping habits before your child is walking and able to run away from you at bedtime or try to climb out of her cot. Bedtime does need to be a peaceful time, particularly if you have a child who is difficult to settle or who has sleep problems.

You can set up a good pre-bedtime pattern by making sure that teatime is about the same time each day and then giving your toddler his bath. He doesn't have to have a bath every day but in my experience it is a good idea, as this becomes part of the bedtime routine and helps your child to unwind at the end of the day. Also toddlers can make a mess with their food and often need a bath! Children normally love to have a bath, and it can be a special family time together.

When you take her out of the bath, wrap her in her towel and put her on your lap and cuddle her, and sing to her if you like. Try to make this time as peaceful as you can in preparation for bedtime. Dress her in her nightclothes and read a story to her, maybe something that she can look at, just to let her relax with you. It's especially important not to wind her up at this time with tickles or exciting games. Then put her in her cot and tuck her in. You may find your toddler has a special cuddly toy in her cot or likes to cuddle a muslin. This is a good idea, as it gives her a sense of security when she goes to bed. Make sure you have a spare cuddly, so that you can put one through the wash. I wouldn't fill her cot with cuddly toys, and of course make sure any toy she has doesn't have any buttons or bits on it that she can chew off. Before you leave the room say prayers with her or talk about your day if this is what you like to do, stroke her head, kiss her goodnight and turn out the light.

Parents often ask me if they should leave a light on in the bedroom, and I would suggest you don't get into a habit of this. If your toddler is happy without a light then don't put it on. He doesn't need it on, but you may find that he starts wanting the light on as he gets older. If he is obviously frightened then leave the landing light on with his door ajar, or put a little nightlight in his room. You will probably find that he settles down, and you may not need to do this for very long.

Don't worry if your child doesn't settle to sleep straight away once you've left the room, particularly as she grows up and becomes more active and aware of her surroundings. She may sing or chat in her cot for 20 minutes or so before she drops off to sleep, and this is perfectly normal. If your child is grizzly and unsettled, go back into the room after a little while and just stroke her head to reassure her, and then leave the room quickly. If at all possible, don't pick her up as this is likely to wake her up and you will have to start the whole winding-down process again.

Older children will often plead for another story or call you back time after time for drinks or questions about things to prolong bedtime. To deal with this, you need to have decided how many stories you'll read and be firm on just going back in once after you've settled your child down.

Should My Toddler Have His Own Room?

There is still quite a debate going on as to where children should sleep. There are different schools of thought on this, and it has to be your decision where your child sleeps. However, I personally feel quite strongly that babies and children should be in their own cot or bed and in their own bedroom wherever possible. This depends on how much room you have, and it is quite acceptable for children to share bedrooms. I know of families in which very young children and babies have slept together and it has worked very well. It is amazing how quickly a toddler will get used to having a baby sibling in the room with him, and they will not wake each other. If your toddler is still in a cot it is important that he can't get out and throw things into the baby's cot or climb in, so be careful from the safety angle. When I grew up as the eldest of six children we shared bedrooms, two of us in each room. As we grew up it was great fun to share, and I think that children benefit from sharing a room. Even if you have the space for each child to have their own room, it is nice for them to perhaps share at some stage if they want to. I believe it's not a good idea for young children to have a television in their rooms, as you don't have control over when they watch it or what they watch.

The main reason I feel that children should not sleep in your bedroom is that you as a couple need your own space together without your toddler. This doesn't mean you don't love her; in fact I think you are doing more for her by moving her out of your bedroom than by letting her in. It is all part of growing up and learning to be apart from you. If your toddler has learnt to be happy settling in her own room, it will make it easier for her to gradually grow in independence. It is lovely to see a toddler happy in her cot in her own bedroom, with her toys around her. The cot really does need to be a happy place where she feels safe. Often I have heard little ones singing and talking in their cots when they wake from sleep, and this is just how it should be. All my children loved their bedrooms, and as they got bigger they would go off to play there when they wanted to be on their own.

If you have had your baby in your room for the first year of his life and you now want him to sleep in his own bedroom, then I would advise you to move him into his own room before he gets much older. At one year old he is quite likely to make a fuss if he is moved into his own room, so be prepared for this. You and your partner will have to be firm and need to have made the decision together; you may find it takes a few nights for your child to settle in his own room. It's a good idea to let him spend time playing with his toys in the new room before you move his cot there, so that it is a place where he feels happy and secure. To make it easier I would move his cot into his new room during the day so he has his daytime sleep in there first. When you come to put him down that night, he will already have had one sleep in there before. If you find that he is very unsettled when you put him in his new room, it's important to go in and comfort him, but do not move him back into your bedroom. You will find that he settles and comes to feel secure in his own bedroom after a few days.

Should I Have My Toddler in My Bed?

What about having your toddler in bed with you – does it matter? I want to say very clearly that I think it is lovely to have your children come into bed with you for cuddles in the morning, but not until you are ready; I don't mean at 5 a.m.! I think there is a place for family time in bed in the morning, especially at weekends. When I go and stay with my grandchildren they bring their books and come into bed with me and have a cuddle and a story before we get dressed. I believe that children never forget these times. I am also aware that this is not what every family wants to do and that it's all right if you don't feel comfortable with all being in the same bed.

I have to say that I am not a great believer in children sleeping in bed with their parents. In general, if your toddler is well, I think she should be in her own cot or bed. Sometimes if your child is ill or very upset you may want to take her into your bed to comfort her, but I would suggest that you put her back in her own bed as soon as she is calm again. It is tempting to take her in with you and snuggle down rather than get up and put her back in her cot. However, children very quickly learn new things and will soon be waking to come into bed with you if you are not careful.

Your child may be sleeping with you because you are still breast-feeding, or because he is unsettled through the night and sleeping with you has become a habit. If your child sleeps with you all the time, you and your partner will not sleep so well, and as your toddler grows and becomes more active he will start pushing you out of bed. Eventually he will need to have his own space and be in his own cot or bed. I feel that the longer you leave moving him out into his own cot or bed, the more difficult it will be for the whole family, and the more unsettled he will be.

If you have been sleeping with your toddler and you decide to move her to her own cot or bed, you will need to have made up your mind to be quite firm about this decision. If your child is going into a cot, she is very likely to cry and make a fuss when you first make the changeover. Make sure that she has her favourite cuddly toy or blanket in the cot with her to help her feel secure. You will need to go in and comfort and reassure her, probably several times before she actually goes to sleep. You may find that this happens for several days until she becomes used to settling in her cot, but she will get there. Stick by your decision and don't be tempted to take her back into bed to help her settle, or you will have to start the whole process again. If your toddler is going into a bed, it is very likely that she will keep getting out and coming downstairs or into your bed. Again, it is most important that you stand by your decision and quietly take her back to her own bed. You will probably have to do this numerous times until your child begins to learn to settle in her own bed.

Daytime Naps

It is important that your child has good daytime naps, as this will enable him to sleep better at night. Napping means that your child will not be completely overtired by teatime and then unable to settle at bedtime. A child who naps and sleeps well will normally eat well and be a generally happy little person.

From the age of twelve to eighteen months, your toddler will still need two naps a day, usually one long nap in the late morning and then a shorter nap in the afternoon. From the age of around eighteen months, you may find that some days she doesn't seem ready for her morning nap, and needs to have an early lunch before her sleep. This is perfectly normal and is a sign that she is ready for her nap times to change. Gradually she will move to having just one long nap a day. The timing of this nap usually gets later as your child gets older, as she can be up for longer stretches of time. However, if she's been awake in the night for whatever reason, she will need earlier naps. If your child has been ill or unsettled in the night or is having a growth spurt, you may well find that she needs longer naps for a few days.

Two Naps a Day

If your child is awake early he will certainly need two naps a day. You will find that by about 10 a.m. he will be rubbing his eyes and ready to go down for a nap. He will probably sleep for about two hours and then have another nap in the afternoon. Try to make this nap short and ensure that he is awake again by 4.30. This will also mean that he is ready for bed at around 7 p.m. As he gets older and sleeps longer at night you will find you can gradually move his nap time to the late morning, ensuring that he has a good sleep, and then he will only need the odd afternoon nap.

Late Morning Nap

In my experience, a toddler who sleeps till around 7 a.m. will not need to go for a nap until about 11.00 or 11.30. For this morning nap, put her in her cot with the curtains drawn – you don't need blackouts – put on her musical toy if she has one, settle her down in the usual way, and leave her to sleep. You may find that she plays with her toys and sings for a little while. Don't worry; this is quite all right, as she is just settling down. She should normally have a very deep sleep, and you may well have to wake her so that she doesn't sleep all the afternoon. However, if she has been awake in the night and is very tired then leave her for longer. Another reason for letting her have a longer sleep is if you want her to stay up later than her normal bedtime because you are taking her out. I usually suggest that you wake her after she has had about two hours' sleep. If you let your child nap until she wakes on her own you will find it difficult to settle her at bedtime, as she will be full of energy and not ready to go to sleep. I nearly always woke my children from their daytime sleep and they were often grumpy for 20 minutes or so, but it was always worth it as they were then ready for bed in the evening.

If you have to wake him, do it gently, as most children really do not like being woken in the day. Go in and talk to him quietly, open the curtains, take his covers off and leave him for a few minutes to come to himself. If he is grumpy and doesn't want to be by himself, get him out of his cot, put him on your lap and give him lots of cuddles. Try not to hurry him. If you are going out then wake him in plenty of time so that he is not rushed. Many children don't want to have their lunch as soon as they have woken up, so give him some time to play with his toys or just have cuddles with you. You will find that once he is wide awake he will probably eat a really good lunch. You may find that he needs another 10- or 15-minute nap at about 4 p.m., otherwise he will fall asleep over his tea.

Lunchtime Nap

Sometimes I find that you can give a child an early lunch at around 11.30 or 12.00 and then put her in her cot for a nap. This works well if she has had her breakfast at around 8 a.m. She will then sleep for a good two hours and be all set for the afternoon. Most toddlers having a nap around this time of the day will not need another nap in the late afternoon. I think you have to find nap times that suit you and your toddler and, of course, be flexible.

Naps Out and About

Your toddler may sleep in the buggy if you are out walking or at the shops. I find that sleeps in the buggy while out shopping are more difficult, as he will be interested in all that is going on around him. However, if he is used to going to the shops for a daily visit then he probably will sleep without any problems in his buggy. If you go out in the car your toddler may nap then, so it can be a good idea to plan journey times around your child's nap times. It is always difficult to keep children awake if they are tired, you have been out to tea and you are going home in the car; they invariably drop off as soon as you start moving. If this happens, do your usual bedtime routine once you get home, making sure you have a good winding-down time, and then put him to bed. You may find that he won't settle quite so quickly as he is not so tired. If you want to keep him up for a little longer this is fine, but don't get into a habit, and try to stick to your normal bedtime routine.

If your toddler is at nursery or with a childminder then she will be used to having her sleep at the same time each day. They will then tell you when her nap time is changing, and you can discuss together how to go about it. Be prepared for some days to be different, though, and if your child is getting overtired and is obviously ready for a sleep, don't make her wait: put her down to nap.

Where Should My Toddler Sleep in the Day?

It is good to be flexible about daytime naps but often it is not easy to settle a toddler in a different place from where he is used to napping. Younger babies are often happy to sleep almost anywhere, and it is good if you can vary where your baby naps during the last few months before he is one year old. The ideal place for the long daytime nap is in his cot, where you can tuck him down and he should sleep well. But this is not always practical and there will be times when you will be out at the shops or with friends and want your toddler to sleep somewhere other than his cot. In general you want your child to be able to settle for his nap in different places and the way to do this is to vary where he sleeps, so that he doesn't get stuck in a rigid routine of always being in the same place for his nap.

My children always had their morning sleep in their cot and they didn't really mind where their afternoon nap was. But this can also be quite a tie, so I would suggest you take her out in her buggy when she is ready for a morning nap and get her to sleep this way. Repeat this several times so she gets used to it. On the other hand, if she has been used to sleeping in her buggy and not in her cot, then stay in for a day or so and put her in her cot until she has got used to it. At weekends be flexible about where she has her daytime nap. If you are visiting friends and they have a cot then try putting her in that. Always make sure you have her favourite cuddly toy or blanket with you, as that will help her to settle in a strange place. If you are going away, invest in a travel cot, then settle her in that when you can so that she gets used to it.

In my experience babies and young children will nearly always sleep in the car, and sleep very well. This is good if you are going out for the day and want your child to have a sleep. Sometimes you will find that he drops off to sleep in the car just as you are arriving at your destination, and you feel it is a pity to wake him when he needs to sleep. If you are parked in a safe area within your home's boundary and he is quite safe, get out of the car quietly, push the door closed and leave him to have a sleep. Make sure that you keep checking that he is all right. Always leave a window open, and remember that a car can get hot very quickly even if the day does not seem hot. You cannot of course do this if you are at the shops or in a place where it is not safe to leave him. NEVER EVER leave a child in a hot car unattended.

Naps and Quiet Times from Two to Three Years

You will find that as your child grows and gets to the age of two to three years she will not be needing so much daytime sleep, especially if she is a good sleeper at night. Some days she will need a good sleep, and then you may find she goes for several days when she doesn't need a sleep at all. When this happens, either she doesn't go in her cot or bed, or if you want some quiet time yourself she can just go for a rest with her picture books. I always feel that if you are at home with your child it is good for her to have half an hour or so of being quiet, either in her room or sitting watching a video or DVD with you. It is good training for her to know how to be quiet and rest. This will enable her to rest and switch off as she gets older. Some children, though, find resting much easier than others and are happy to stop for a while. You may have a child who rushes round madly all the time and doesn't want to stop. I think it is good if you can gently teach her to sit and be quiet at times, either with books or a video or DVD.

By the time a child is three years old he will mostly be happy just to have a quiet time at some stage during the day. Although he may not need to sleep, it can be good for him to have some time during the day resting on his bed with books and cuddly toys. He should be sleeping well at night, although you may find that sometimes he wakes frightened and distressed from a bad dream. I think that from the age of about two years it is normal for children to dream, and it is very real to them.

Sleep Problems

Many parents I meet have a real fear of their toddler not settling at night or waking in the night on a long-term basis. We all need to have a good night's sleep and want to ensure that our children settle and sleep well. As I travel around, I see that sleep problems can become a big issue within a family and cause huge stress between parents as they become increasingly exhausted. You may be reading this wishing that you had got your toddler into a good sleep pattern earlier. However, don't despair: you will need to persevere with a good routine and be quite firm, but it can be done.

Refusing to Settle to Sleep in the Evening

For some families, bedtime can become a battleground, with parents feeling they have to bribe their child from teatime onwards in order to get her into bed. These constant battles end up with the child exhausted and the parents stressed, and the situation can feel quite out of control. Bedtime is anything but calm and happy and can take hours, meaning that children are losing out on sleep and often waking at night because they have become so unsettled.

The first approach to these problems is to ensure that you have a good evening and bedtime routine. Make sure that teatime is around the same time every day, if possible introduce a relaxing bathtime, and have a peaceful winding-down time with a story. I often advise families who are having this kind of struggle to begin the whole evening routine half an hour earlier to make sure that their child is not overtired at the start of the bedtime wind-down. One of the things I have also found useful over the years is to distract the child's attention from the battle, either by telling him a story or by talking about all the fun things that you have done together during the day. It's surprising how often this works, and while you're doing this you will find that you can undress a child and get him into the bath and he will hardly have noticed. You will also need to be absolutely clear and have made up your mind that you are going to end these battles. It's amazing how once you take this decision your child somehow senses that you mean business. It is essential to keep calm and not raise your voice; tell your child what you are expecting him to do next, and if he doesn't respond in a positive way, pick him up and take him upstairs without making a lot of fuss. Don't have lots of dialogue.

To prepare your toddler for going to bed when she's had long enough in the bath, distract her attention by chatting or singing. If she pleads to stay in the bath longer and you want to get on with bedtime, just calmly say 'no' and then take her out, wrap her in a towel and put her on your lap. This is the time to have lots of cuddles. Dress her in her nightclothes, read her a story and put her in her cot or bed. Try to gently move from one stage to the next without too much fuss. Quite often your toddler will scream and shout because she doesn't want to be put down in bed. If she's in a cot, gently say goodnight to her, stroke her head and tell her she's not coming out because it's night-night time, and leave the room. If she's still shouting, leave her for as long as you feel you can before you go back into the room. Reassure her by stroking her head and again tell her that it's sleep time. Leave the room without engaging in a debate or taking her out of her cot. If she's in a bed and keeps getting out, just keep quietly taking her back and putting her in bed, telling her it's sleep time but not getting into a dialogue. You may need to do this several times; in fact it can go on all evening until she finally falls asleep. You may have to follow this sleep training for several nights until she gets used to going to bed and settling herself without any fuss.

Wanting to Be Settled by the Same Person

Sometimes a toddler goes though a stage of wanting only one parent to put him to bed. This can be upsetting for the other parent and make them feel very left out. Don't worry if this happens, as it is quite normal. Sometimes it will happen if Dad has been working away for a while and Mum has been the main carer. It may happen if Mum has been into hospital and had another baby, and Dad or Grandma has been doing bedtime. The best thing to do is not to make a fuss about it but to pretend you haven't noticed. Gradually try to share the role of bedtime so that your child forgets his need for one particular parent. Try not to be upset about this, as your child does not love one parent any less by wanting the other parent to do bedtime. You will find that if you are patient and loving your child will soon be happy with either of you putting him to bed.

Wanting a Dummy or Pacifier

I am not a great advocate of dummies, as at some stage you will have to take them away. The longer your child has a dummy, the more difficult it can be to take it away, as it will become her sleep-time comforter. First, I would take it away for her daytime sleeps so she gets used to not having it. She may make a fuss but you can try to distract her attention by giving her a toy to take to bed with her. You could introduce a muslin or cuddly at sleep times; this stays in the cot for naps and night-times. Be firm and stick to the idea of her not having the dummy for her sleep. When you have mastered the daytime sleep then take the dummy away when she goes to bed at night. You may well find that this is easier to do than it was for the daytime sleep as she is getting used to settling without it.

Waking in the Night

Your child may have been a very good sleeper and have been sleeping through the night since an early age, then suddenly start waking for no apparent reason. This comes as rather a shock, as you felt you had got a really good sleeper. It is perfectly normal for young children to wake at night from time to time, and even to have a spell of bad nights, so don't think you have done something wrong. Children who have learnt to fall asleep without a parent being with them are much more likely to go back to sleep on their own when they wake in the night. All babies and children wake from time to time in the night or come into a lighter sleep, but not all of them wake right up and shout. Sometimes they will call out or talk in their sleep and then settle again on their own, especially if they have been in a good sleep pattern from an early age. When your child wakes in the night it is a good idea to check him if he doesn't just grumble and go back to sleep, as he may have got his legs or arms caught in the bars of the cot. You can look round the door but don't let him see you, because if he does that may disturb him. Obviously, if he is stuck go in and straighten him out, tuck him in without saying anything, and leave the room.

There are a number of reasons why a baby will wake in the night. She may wake because of teething or illness or if she is cold or too hot. She may also wake because she has a wet or dirty nappy. A toddler will often wake in the night when a new baby comes. I have found when I am working in homes with a new baby that invariably the toddler will have a period of waking at night and being quite distressed, simply because of the huge change in her life. Toddlers are growing in every way and taking in everything that is going on around them, so they will very often be unsettled if things are different at home. You may have moved house or there may have been an upset or a change in family life. Mummy may have gone back to work or Daddy is working away; maybe Daddy used to do bedtime and your toddler is upset that he is not around for this. Bigger changes such as bereavement or parental separation can also have a huge effect on your child's sleeping.

Waking at night may be a habit. Babies and young children can very quickly form a habit of waking at night, particularly if you get them up and give them a bottle and make them think, 'This is fun!' You may have been away for a few days' holiday together and come home to find that they won't settle or that they wake in the night. The consolation is to remember that we all as parents have broken nights and it is how we deal with them that matters. In the next sections we'll look at the different problem areas and what we can do about them.

Teething

When your toddler is a year old she will probably have cut her front eight teeth, and the rest of her teeth will come through over the next few months. She will show the usual signs of teething and may run a slight temperature too, and she will certainly wake at night sometimes with the pain. Go to her, put teething granules or teething gel on her gums, reassure her, and give her a drink if you think she needs it. It is also perfectly acceptable to give her a dose of a paracetamol preparation for babies or children if she needs it. Try to leave her in her cot if you can, because when you take her out she may not want to go back in. In my experience it is easier to settle a child in her cot if she is not too upset. Of course, if she is very distressed, get her out. She will need to be cuddled and comforted before you put her back in.

Illness

Your child will wake if he is going down with an illness or if he is feeling unwell, either with a high fever or a tummy bug. Ear infections are quite common in young children, and chest infections and asthma can also keep young children awake. If your child suffers from eczema this can be uncomfortable for him at night. Make sure that you go to him when he wakes; he may need you to get him out of his cot and he may need to be cuddled and given more medication, depending on what illness he has. Of course, if you are seriously worried about his condition you must call your general practitioner or take him to the hospital accident and emergency department. If your child has been in hospital or has had a serious illness then he may be wakeful at night. If this is the case, you will need to be patient and very loving with him and gradually teach him that night-time is for sleeping and that you are still there with him.

Waking from Cold or Heat

It is quite common for children to wake from being too cold, especially if the temperature outside suddenly drops in the night. Toddlers will often wriggle out from under their covers and get cold. You can put your toddler in a type of sleeping bag that keeps children warm and prevents them waking from cold. If the weather is very cold then you may need to put a heater in the bedroom to keep the temperature at an even level. Don't let the room get too hot, though; 18°C (65°F) is about the right temperature. When the weather is hot make sure your child does not have too much night clothing on, or she may wake from being uncomfortably hot.

Waking for a Nappy Change

Your child may wake because his nappy is very wet or dirty. If this happens then change his nappy in his cot and settle him down again as quickly as you can. Don't say much to him, just kiss him goodnight and leave the room. Most children who are good sleepers will settle quickly after having their nappy changed. Toddlers will often wake early in the morning because they have a dirty nappy; then, of course, they think it is time to get up!

Light Levels and Noise

A toddler can become suddenly conscious of light and dark and will sometimes wake because she is frightened. She then needs to be reassured, and you may find that a light on outside her bedroom door or in her room will help her to feel secure. Sometimes she will wonder where you are and want to be reassured that you are not far away. Your child may be waking from noise; usually this is outside noise, and maybe something you cannot do anything about. You need to go to her and reassure her that you are there, and in time she will get used to it.

Overtiredness

Toddlers can wake in the night because they are overtired. They will go off to sleep when you put them to bed, then a couple of hours later they will wake screaming. If you think your toddler is not going to settle himself, go in to him, talk quietly and tell him you love him, cuddle and reassure him, tuck him in again and leave the room. If he doesn't settle, leave him for ten minutes or so and then go in again and repeat the process. You may find you have to do this several times before he settles to sleep again. Once he has gone into a deep sleep he will probably sleep well till the morning. Extreme overtiredness can feed poor sleeping habits, leading to a child waking regularly at night, not sleeping well during the day, and perhaps even showing destructive and angry behaviour. To prevent overtiredness, make sure you give him a good sleep during the day, start bedtime earlier before he gets too tired and have a good winding-down time. Read several stories to him if he is very wound up. I find stories are better than television, as anything too visual doesn't help him to wind down.

Life Changes

Any sort of family disturbance such as your partner leaving you, a parent going back to work or a house move can cause a young child to wake distressed in the night. Again, show lots of love and cuddles and spend time at bedtime reassuring her you are there. When she wakes in the night spend time just cuddling her and telling her you love her. Always make sure she has her favourite toy in her cot or bed with her, and her cuddly if she has one.

New Baby

I have worked with lots of families in which the mother coming home from hospital with a new baby has meant that after two or three days the toddler starts waking in the night and is very distressed. This is quite a shock to parents, particularly if the child has been a good sleeper. The most important thing is to show patience even when you are tired. It is difficult when you are up in the night feeding the newborn and just as you settle back to sleep your toddler wakes screaming his head off. When this goes on night after night you all become exhausted and wonder when it will end. Your toddler will settle down again but it may take a week or so. When this happens, try not to be tempted to take your toddler into bed with you; this is so easy to do, just to get a good night. But if you do this it will be more difficult to get him to settle in his own bed again at night. The best thing to do is to get up and go into his room. If he is in a cot then comfort him with cuddles and reassurance that you are there. If he is very distressed get him out and put him on your lap, but don't take him out of his bedroom if you can help it. Calm him down on your lap, give him a little drink if this helps and put him back in his cot, stroking his head and telling him you love him. You may find he settles back to sleep for the rest of the night. If he does not settle at all, leave him for a little while and go back in to him. Don't take him out of his cot this time; just reassure him, stroke his head, speak gently to him and leave the room.

You may find this goes on for several nights, and it really is exhausting, but try to remember that it is only for a time and she will grow through it. Her world has been upset by another little person coming into her family and taking Mummy's time and attention. If your child is in a bed then she may well keep running out of her room into yours. This is more difficult to deal with as you will need to keep getting out of bed to take her back and put her in her bed. Use the same method as I described above for a cot. Most importantly, try to get some rest in the day if you are having broken nights like this.

Bad Dreams

When a child gets to the age of around two it is quite common for him to have a bad dream or nightmare. He may be very distressed and still asleep, although he appears awake. You need to comfort him, cuddle him and talk quietly to him, again reassuring him that you are there. He may quieten quickly and you can then tuck him back into his bed, but you may need to sit with him for a little while as he dozes off to sleep again. If he is in a bed he may get out and walk around in his sleep. This can be very disconcerting for you if he does it in the middle of the night and you hear noises in the house. Make sure he cannot fall downstairs or get into the kitchen or anywhere where he can come to harm if you don't hear him. Usually children who sleepwalk go to their parents' bedroom first. Comfort and cuddle him and put him back to bed, and again you may need to sit with him for a little while as he settles back to sleep. If your child is very anxious at bedtime, try spending some time with him and reassuring him that we all need to rest and we go to bed so that we're ready to do fun things the next day.

Climbing Out of the Cot

You may find that your toddler tries to climb out of his cot. If he is a big child he will probably be able to do this and could hurt himself. Make sure he doesn't have lots of toys in his cot that he can pile up and climb on and topple over the side. If he does get out and you find you can't keep him in, then it is probably time you looked at putting him in a bed. Alternatively, you could put a mattress by his cot so that if he does get out he will roll onto that first. Make sure there is nothing in his room that he can hurt himself with: take away any toys or objects that are not safe.

Waking for Drinks or Food

Many parents ask me if they should give their child a drink in the night if she wakes. I don't have a problem with this as long as it doesn't become a habit. It is a good idea to give drinks out of a cup at night, even if she is still on the breast or bottle. If your child wakes and is distressed and having a drink helps to calm her down, then of course give her one. If your child is ill then she will probably need to drink, especially if she has a high fever. I would only give water in the night and not juice, as it is bad for teeth and encourages decay. If she is waking in the night because of teething or feeling unwell, then make sure you have the medicines and a drink nearby so that you haven't got to go downstairs in the middle of the night.

I would not give snacks at all at night, as in my experience this habit can be difficult to break. If your child is eating well there is no reason for her to eat in the night. Even if she is going through a stage of not eating during the day, it is not a good idea to fill her up with snacks in the night, as this is likely to make the problem worse in the day.

Waking for a Bottle or Breast-feed in the Night

Many parents I talk to are concerned that their toddler will only settle with a feed and then wakes continuously through the night for more. When this happens, a toddler's appetite during the day will be affected, as he fills up on milk on and off during the night. What can you do if your toddler is still waking for night feeds? The first thing I would say is that he doesn't need these feeds. You need to establish how you are going to drop these feeds and help him to sleep right through the night. First, you and your partner must decide together that you mean business and are *not* going to give a night feed. Once you have made that decision somehow it all becomes easier. When your toddler wakes in the night, leave him for five minutes if you can, then go in to him, stroke his head and tell him gently but definitely that he is not coming out as it is night-night time, then leave the room. The most important thing is not to get him out of his cot. You will no doubt have to repeat this process several times and he may become quite upset, but stick with it if you can. You will find that he will go back to sleep, and when it happens the next night he will not shout for so long. You will find that after a few nights he will sleep right through and you will be very pleased with yourselves. This is the method I would use whether you are breast- or bottle-feeding.

Waking Early in the Morning

At some stage, I think all children wake early in the morning and want to come out of their cots or beds and start the day. Some children have always woken early, so that parents are run ragged after a while and don't know what to do. Sometimes children will wake because of noise in the house or outside. Some will wake earlier in the summer time because of the dawn light, and some will just wake because they are all set to start the day long before you are. If your child is not well then she may wake early but that is quite understandable, as she may need to be comforted or have a drink. Some toddlers will wake early because they have a dirty nappy; in fact lots of children do a poo early in the morning and then stand up in their cot and shout. If your child has been a really good sleeper and suddenly starts waking before 7 a.m., don't worry; it is perfectly normal. What you don't want is for this to become a habit.

So how do we deal with early morning waking? I would make sure that if you have been using blackout blinds in your child's bedroom, you make the room slightly lighter. The reason for this is that when he wakes in the morning he can see where he is. Don't make it too light, though. I would leave a few special toys in his cot when you check him last thing at night so that when he wakes in the morning he has something to look at and play with. Make sure all these toys are safe, and leave a picture book or two in the cot as well. It may be a good idea to keep these toys just for his cot so that they are fresh to him every morning. When he wakes, and if it is not time for him to be up yet, leave him for five to ten minutes if you can. Then if he is having a good shout go in to him and tell him quietly that it is not time to get up yet and he has to stay in his cot till Mummy and Daddy are ready to get up. You may have to keep going back to him, using the same method you use for controlled crying (see pp. 63–64). It does mean that you are going to be in and out of bed for a while, and this may happen for several days. This method does work well, and I have been with families where I have given this advice and they have been thrilled to see that after a few days their child is quiet even though he may be awake. Often you will find that your child may wake, talk and play for a while, then go back to sleep. You might even have to go in and wake him to get him up.

If your child is in a bed and continually comes into your room before it is time to get up, then I would suggest you get an alarm clock. There is a lovely one available with a rabbit's face on, with ears that lift up when it is time to get up. Set the clock for a time that you feel is reasonable for your child to be up and about and explain to her that until the bunny wakes with his ears up she must stay in her room. Also leave some toys and books on the bed for her so that she can snuggle into bed with them when she wakes. Of course, you have to be the ones who say what time is acceptable for your child to get up. When our children were in their cots I would get them up at 8 a.m. each day, and that was a way of life to them. I know that today many mothers work and their toddlers go into a day nursery, so they have to be up long before this. You will normally find that if your child has been a good sleeper and starts waking early you will be able to sort the problem out quite quickly. If you are up early during the week, try to train your child to stay in her cot or bed for longer at the weekend so that you are all able to sleep in for a while.

Travelling or Changing Time Zones

If you are travelling the world with your toddler and going in and out of different time zones, this too will upset his sleeping habits. If you are staying in the same time zone for a while then I would put him straight into that zone when you get there. You may well find that he has to have an extra nap in the day or stay up a little later at night until he gets used to it. It is a good idea to wake him at breakfast time so that he can start the day with you, but you may find you need to be flexible on this depending on how far the time zone is from the one you have just left. The important thing is to be flexible with him, especially if you are on holiday. If he is grumpy because of different nap times or because he hasn't had enough sleep at night, then put him down in his cot or bed for a nap. It is miserable for little children to have to keep going when they are exhausted.

Long-term Sleep Problems

In all of these sleeping issues that we have talked about, it is most important for you as parents to be able to cope. Sleep deprivation does strange things to us, and we can become very unbalanced in the way we view things. Having worked with babies and young children over the years and having had my own family, I know how broken nights can affect your health. Long-term sleep deprivation can affect your mental state, so it is important to get help from your doctor. Sometimes it is difficult to sleep even when your child has settled down into good sleeping habits, as you have become overtired and your brain just will not switch off at night. It is then that you may well need sleeping tablets from your doctor to help you to relax and sleep well at night again. There are also some very good herbal and natural sleeping remedies that can help you to relax.

Sleep Training

Many people ask me about sleep training and how long they can let their toddler shout for, or whether they can just leave her. If you are doing sleep training and your child is well, fit and healthy, then a good shout won't hurt her. I prefer not to put a time limit on it as every parent is different, and some feel able to leave their children for longer than others. However, if you are sleep training you will have to let her shout for a little while, as that is part of learning to settle herself. Obviously a toddler is going to make much more noise than a young baby and will also be able to pull herself up in her cot and stand holding onto the bars and shouting.

I meet many parents as I travel around who tell me their toddler has never slept through the night and wonder if they are too late to do sleep training. If this applies to you, take heart. It is never too late to start; it is just rather more difficult with an older child. First, you and your partner need to have made up your minds that you are going to have a plan and stick with it, because I can assure you it always works; it just takes time. You need to choose a time when you don't have family or friends staying and when you are not going to be highly stressed with work, so you can concentrate on sleep training. If you are having battles with daytime naps as well as night sleeping, then I would certainly concentrate on getting daytime naps sorted out first, following the advice given earlier in this chapter. For older children, it can be a good idea to have a reward chart for good sleeping. This will often encourage them to settle and to stay in bed, as you can talk about 'good sleeping' with them and what rewards they will earn.

Controlled Crying

There are two methods for sleep training that you can use. One is controlled crying and the other is 'shout it out' (or 'cold turkey'). Controlled crying will take longer than 'shout it out', but it is a gentler way of sleep training for you as a parent. Controlled crying is when you go in to your child when he wakes, having left him to shout for as long as you feel comfortable with. This may be two minutes, five minutes or ten minutes. You may find that by leaving him for a few minutes he will settle, but if he has been used to being picked up every time he shouts then he will not settle easily. In controlled crying, when you feel you have left him for long enough, go into his room, reassure him, stroke his head and face and tell him you love him, tuck him in if he is out of his blankets or duvet and leave the room. Most importantly, don't get him out of his cot. He is very likely to shout as soon as you have gone. Leave him for longer this time, and then go back into his room and do the same thing again. Each time he shouts leave him for slightly longer, and repeat the process. You may find that the first night you are in and out of his room nearly all night, but he will settle. This may take several nights, but I assure you it will work. Within a week he should be sleeping through the night and you will be thrilled.

Shout It Out

The 'shout it out' method is just as it sounds; for a few nights you'll need to be tough and leave your child to shout once you have put her down to sleep. Always go in once to tell her she is not coming out of her cot as it is bedtime. Stroke her head, tell her mummy loves her and leave the room. This will also apply if she wakes in the night. It is most important to check that your toddler has not got herself caught in the bars of the cot and that she is safe; just look around the door so that she cannot see you. When all goes quiet and you think she has settled, go in and check her again.

Some children will be sick after a period of shouting, and this is very upsetting. You need to clean him up, give him a cuddle without making a fuss about it or talking about him having been sick, and put him back into his cot. The important thing is to show him in a loving way that he has to sleep at night. Whether your child has slept well beforehand and is going through a time of bad sleeping or whether he has never slept through the night, try to remember that it is only for a time and you can work through it using the right methods.

Moving from a Cot to a Bed

When Should I Move My Toddler into a Bed?

All children at some stage will need to be moved out of their cot, as they will grow too big for it and will also need the freedom of being in a bed. It is all part of growing up and can be made great fun for your toddler. Usually a good time to move your toddler into a bed is at about two years of age, but as some cots are very large, some parents don't move their child into a bed until she is around three. Sometimes you will find she has started getting out of her cot, and this may be a sign that she is ready to go into a bed. If you have a new baby or are going to have a baby then it is a good idea to plan your toddler's move so that it doesn't coincide with the baby's birth. If you are going to need her cot for another baby, try to move her out of the cot about a month to six weeks before you expect the baby to come. This way she will get used to her bed and not feel she is being pushed out because of the baby. If she is not quite ready for a bed then I would leave her in her cot for a couple of months after the baby is born. It can be exciting for her, as she is giving her cot to the baby, and she is a big girl going into a bed of her own.

How Do I Move My Toddler from a Cot to a Bed?

When you move your toddler into a bed you can do it either by putting him into his bed for daytime naps and into his cot at night for a while, if you have room in his bedroom for a cot and a bed. The other way to do it is to take his cot away, put all his cuddly toys and favourite things into his bed and put him in it for his daytime sleep first; then he can sleep in his bed at night too. You can buy bars that slip under the mattress and act as a protection against him falling out of bed. I think these are a good idea, as they help him to feel secure and may stop him from getting out of bed all the time. You may find you need to keep putting him back to bed again and again until he learns to stay put. Just like his cot has been, make sure bed is a happy place for him to be. One way to help him feel excited about his new bed is to let him choose his own special bed linen.

Top Ten Tips for Good Sleeping

- *Get plenty of fresh air and exercise during the day.*
- *Eat well.*
- *Have good daytime naps.*
- *Have an early evening wind-down time.*
- *Don't sleep in parents' bedroom.*
- *Have a structured bedtime routine.*
- *Be in bed by 7 p.m.*
- *Reassure him, but don't get your child up if he wakes in the night.*
- *Don't be afraid to settle him back if he wakes too early.*
- *Maintain a calm home environment.*

CHAPTER 5

Feeding Your Toddler

Over the years as I've worked with young families I have come across many parents who are worried about their children's eating habits. Problems such as not wanting to eat or being very fussy about food can start quite early on in a child's life. In this chapter I hope to allay some of these fears about eating problems and talk about how we can encourage our young children to eat and make mealtimes an enjoyable and fun time.

As I look back over the years to my own childhood I see an amazing change in our eating habits, some of them for the better but, sadly, some of them for the worse. Years ago there was very little choice, particularly after the Second World War, when food rationing was still part of daily life in Britain. It was normal for families to have the same menu week in and week out. Thankfully this has changed and we now have a wonderful variety of foods that we are able to buy, not only from our own countries but from all over the world. I feel sometimes though that we have too much choice today and the pendulum has swung the other way, so that we overwhelm our children with too many alternatives.

The thing I feel most sad about is that many families no longer sit down to eat together. When I was young we had all our meals together as a family and there was never any question of eating food on our laps in front of the television. I believe that sitting round the table together as a family and enjoying our food as a natural part of the day helps to encourage good eating habits. Mealtimes are a great time to catch up and chat as a family. As your children get older, mealtimes are an opportunity for them to tell you about their day, especially if they have had problems at school. Children will often relax over a meal and open up and tell you things that they might find difficult to express without the space and togetherness of a family mealtime. It is important to teach your children from an early age that food is to be enjoyed and that it is perfectly normal to eat and take time over a meal. Introducing this into your child's day at an early age builds the foundations for good eating habits.

Encouraging Your Toddler to Enjoy Food

I feel it is important to introduce lots of different foods and tastes in the first year of your child's life. I have found that children who are introduced to solid food later rather than earlier can become fussy over different tastes. I am also a great believer in making mealtimes enjoyable so that your child looks forward to coming to the table to eat.

So how do we encourage our children to eat well? By the time your child is a year old you will know what he likes and what he dislikes. There are certain foods that children may not like very much, such as leeks, onions, Brussels sprouts, tomatoes, lettuce and citrus fruits. I would advise you not to push him to eat these foods, but to introduce them again maybe in a week or so. If he is still not very happy you can sometimes mix them in with a food you know he likes, and that way he will probably eat them. I often find that giving small portions encourages children to eat, rather than piling a plate high with so much food that the child feels overwhelmed by what he sees. The same applies when giving him finger food on his tray: give him small amounts so that he eats these first and then he can have some more. This also teaches him that wasting food is not something you are happy about.

It is also important to make food look attractive and tasty. Most toddlers will enjoy little sandwiches cut into shapes with biscuit cutters, or foods made into faces on their plates. If you find cooking difficult, now is the time to try some simple children's recipes that are easy and fun to make. This will encourage you to do more and become more adventurous with cooking. Annabel Karmel has written some very good children's cookery books, and Nigella Lawson has a good section on feeding children in her book *How to Eat*.

Before my children were old enough to help with cooking, I used to put them in their high chair in the kitchen with some toys on the tray and they would sit and watch me cook. Once you feel confident that your child is ready to stand on a chair and help you cook, it's great fun to encourage her to mix things or have little tastes of what you are cooking. Try to involve your child when you are getting a meal ready so that she can see what you are doing. She can help you wash the vegetables, then stir the food as you are making things. Try to make it fun so as to encourage her in the kitchen, as this will help her to see that food is fun and enjoyable.

It's important to set aside time for meals and encourage your child to sit at the table to eat, as this allows him to concentrate on enjoying his food.

While he is still in his high chair it is fairly easy, as you have him strapped in and he can't go anywhere; however, things can become more difficult when he is sitting at the table on a chair, as he can easily get down and run off to play. I would suggest that when he's grown out of his high chair and he sits at the table, you put some straps round him to encourage him to sit still and not jump up and down. It is much easier and less stressful to prevent rather than cure. He will then learn quickly that he sits at the table to have his food. If you're eating at the same time as your child, it's great to chat about what you're having and make lots of 'yummy' noises as you show you're enjoying food too.

Toddlers' Nutritional Needs

For steady growth and development, your child needs a good balanced diet. However, I would advise you not to try to calculate how many calories she is having, whether she is having enough vitamins and minerals and so on, or you will go mad trying to work it out. A good balanced diet for your child will consist of dairy products such as milk, yoghurt and cheese, plenty of fresh fruit and vegetables, cereals, meat and fish, bread and pasta. Your child should not have too much fatty or fried food; it is best to grill her food rather than fry it. Also, ready-made convenience foods are not good for her to have as her staple diet as they often have high levels of salt and preservatives. Children do need salt in their diet, but most food contains enough natural salt to meet these requirements. As a general rule, don't add salt to your child's food, but don't be afraid to add flavour with spices, herbs and sauces to make food tasty. In moderation, it's nice for your child to have some jam or honey on her bread and occasional ice creams, biscuits or cakes. It's easy to get hung up on not allowing your children to have sweet things, but as part of a healthy, balanced diet I believe that it's enjoyable for children to have some treats.

Many parents worry that their child is not drinking enough milk. Toddlers ideally need to have around a pint of full-fat (not skimmed or semi-skimmed) milk a day in drinks, on cereal and in cooking. Some children do go off milk as a drink quite early but don't worry if this happens, as you can make sure that they get plenty of calcium by giving other calcium-rich foods such as yoghurt, cheese, oily fish and green vegetables.

Many parents wonder whether they should give their child a vitamin supplement. In general a well-balanced diet should provide all the vitamins and minerals your toddler needs; however, I have found that giving a supplement of vitamin C in the winter can be good for preventing coughs and colds.

Family Mealtimes

Many families today find it hard to make time to sit down and have family meals together on a regular basis, as working hours are long, parents are often tired, and it can be so much easier to sit with a takeaway or convenience meal on your lap in front of the television. The introduction of unhealthy snacks has also been a reason why children will not sit down and eat properly at the table, as they are so full of crisps and sweets that they don't want a meal. This can be part of a vicious circle: you're worried as a parent that your child is not eating enough at mealtimes, so you give snacks throughout the day to make sure he is having some food, and before long you find he is calling the tune on what and when he eats.

I cannot stress enough the importance of having family mealtimes together. I know that this is not always practical, but the more you can do this the better it will be for you all as a family, even if it is just once or twice a week. Your child will grow up knowing this is a family time, it will help her to feel secure and it will also encourage her to eat well as she sees you enjoying your food. As she gets older it will become a real time of sharing together. I remember the fun and laughter we had at family meals when our children were growing up , especially when our youngest was in a high chair and the older ones would laugh at what she did or was trying to say. You may find that during the working week it is difficult to all sit down to the table together for meals, although you may find you can all have breakfast together. Teatime may be difficult to have together as your child will probably eat earlier than you. At the weekend when you have more time, having lunch together works really well. You could have friends round for lunch with their children too, which helps to make it a good social occasion. This could be anything from a traditional Sunday roast to a big pasta dish or a simple salad and sandwiches; it really doesn't matter what you have – the important thing is to eat together as a family. I can assure you that you will look back on these times with happy memories. As your child gets older, family meals are a good time to teach her some table manners, which will stay with her for life. Having family meals together enables your child to learn about eating with other people and means that you can take her out to a restaurant or to friends' houses for a meal without worrying that she will not behave well.

Helping Your Toddler to Feed Himself

Your toddler will have been having finger food on his high chair tray and will probably have been trying to feed himself with a spoon well before he was a year old. To encourage him to feed himself, let him hold a spoon while you feed him. This means that in between his spoonfuls you can put some food in his mouth too. If you are having problems with your young toddler eating, you will often find that giving him his own spoon encourages him to eat, and you soon find he has had a good meal. To teach him to use his spoon, help him to load it up and steer it into his mouth. You will find that he doesn't always get it right and it may well end up in his ear. But give him time – his co-ordination is still a bit shaky and it will take him a while to get it right. Give him lots of praise when he gets the spoon in and this will encourage him to try again. Gradually let him load the spoon himself as he develops co-ordination. As he gets older you can give him a little set of his own child-size cutlery, and he will probably learn to use the spoon and fork quite quickly, although you will still need to cut his food up.

From around eighteen months onwards mealtimes can become a bit of a battle, as she wants to do all the feeding herself and most likely is not really able to do it all properly. Also you may find she starts throwing her food around, smearing it into her hair or suddenly tipping her plate off her tray onto the floor. You need to be quick and watch what she is up to. Don't leave her unattended with a plate of food or drink, as when your back is turned she may well pitch it all on the floor. When children first do this it is very easy to laugh, and of course they then think it is rather clever and will do it again. Also they are pushing the boundaries and they are fascinated to see their food all round the kitchen floor. You will feel that you're saying 'no' a lot at this stage and may wonder whether she'll ever learn, but persevere and decide what behaviour is acceptable to you as parents at mealtimes.

Mealtime Ideas

I've given some suggestions below of the sort of food your toddler should be having on a regular basis. I hope this will give you some ideas and inspiration for balanced, healthy meals for your child.

Ideas for Breakfast

- *bowl of cereal or porridge*
- *scrambled egg, boiled egg or bacon*
- *toast or bread and butter with jam, Marmite or honey on it*
- *fresh fruit or yoghurt (you can make this into a smoothie)*
- *milk or water or juice to drink.*

For some children, breakfast is the best meal of the day, so your toddler may eat all of the above, which will set him up really well for the day. Don't worry, though, if your child prefers only cereal and a drink. It's perfectly all right at this age to introduce your child to different drinks such as tea (you may prefer decaffeinated or herbal).

Ideas for Lunch

- *casseroles or roast meats*
- *gravy or sauces if needed*
- *pies such as shepherd's pie or fish pie*
- *bakes such as lasagne or moussaka*
- *sausages or vegetarian alternatives*
- *potatoes, rice or couscous*
- *vegetables, either as finger food, mashed, steamed or roast*
- *salad such as cherry tomatoes or cucumber (many children don't like leafy salads)*
- *dessert such as yoghurt, fruit or ice cream*
- *home-made pudding such as crumble or fruit pie*
- *water or juice to drink.*

I've normally found that toddlers will eat a better meal at lunchtime than at teatime, so it is a good idea to give your child her main meal in the middle of the day. She is often too tired to eat a large meal at teatime and will manage better with sandwiches or a light meal before she goes to bed. However, if you do prefer to give your toddler her main meal at teatime, you can give her sandwiches at lunchtime instead.

Ideas for Tea

- *pasta dishes*
- *quiche or sandwiches*

- *baked beans on toast*
- *scrambled or boiled egg or eggy bread*
- *cheese dishes such as cauliflower or macaroni cheese*
- *fish fingers or fish cakes*
- *cold ham or sausage rolls*
- *cherry tomatoes, cucumber, raw carrot or celery*
- *fresh fruit or yoghurt, or dried fruit such as raisins*
- *occasional treats such as cake or pastries*
- *milk, juice, tea or water to drink.*

Remember not to overwhelm your toddler with too many different sorts of food on his plate, as often this encourages him to play with his food rather than eat it. It's better to offer small portions of a couple of foods and then give him more once he's finished. You will need to go on cutting up your toddler's food into small, manageable pieces for quite a while so that he doesn't choke.

Eating at Nursery or Away from Home

During the toddler years, your child may well be going to nursery or to a childminder. It is a good idea to talk to your child's carer about what she is going to have to eat during the day, and at the end of the day to find out what and how much she's eaten so that you know what she needs at teatime. Most nurseries and childminders will be very happy to fill you in, and many keep a record of what each child has eaten. If your child has any food allergies or very specific likes or dislikes, make sure you share these with your child's carer.

I've often noticed that children who are fussy with their food at home eat a better meal when they are with other children in a nursery or with a childminder. Similarly, some children will eat much better with their nanny than with their parents. If your child is going to a childminder or a friend or relative's house for the day, it can help to take along his own bowl, spoon and cup from home to help him feel secure. On the other hand, some children enjoy having different and 'special' bowls and cutlery when they're away from home.

If you're taking your child out to a restaurant or cafe, it's a good idea to have a travel high chair just in case the restaurant doesn't provide them. Some restaurants provide crayons and paper for children to draw on while they are waiting for their meal, which is a great idea. Always take something with you to occupy your toddler while you're waiting for your meal. You will probably find that many restaurants provide suitable food for your toddler, and often a special children's menu, so you don't need to bring your own food from home.

Healthy Snacks

Having a mid-morning snack is a good idea as long as your child is eating well. If she has had breakfast at about 7.30–8 a.m. she will need something mid-morning. Give her a drink of milk, juice or water and a healthy snack, which can be raw fruit or vegetables. Most children enjoy any tasty fruit such as apples, grapes, pears, nectarines or peaches. Some children love raw carrot or celery, but make sure it is cut into pieces that they can eat easily. I think it is good for children to have biscuits and cake from time to time too. I believe that if you don't allow your child to have any sweet treats at all, this can become an issue, as when she is old enough to get them herself she may gorge on them. Or she may be incredibly fussy and look on all sweet foods as bad and something to be avoided at all costs.

Afternoon snacks are fine if your child has had an early lunch and tea is going to be late, but I have found that too many snacks in the afternoon can spoil the appetite for tea. If your child has an early tea and plays after tea, you may well find he is hungry before bed. If this is the case then it is a good idea to let him have a bowl of cereal or a piece of fruit to fill him up. Children always sleep better on a full stomach. He can have a drink too, but remember, when you are starting to train him to be dry at night, to let him drink plenty in the day and then cut his fluid intake down later, not letting him drink after 6 p.m. It's best not to give crisps, chocolate bars or sweets before bedtime, and if he does have a snack remember that he needs to clean his teeth before he goes to bed.

Some parents use snacks as a useful distraction if they are out somewhere and want their child to be quiet. This is fine but try not to let it become a habit so that you always rely on this method. Try distracting her with a story or a special toy that you take with you when you go out. If you're going on a journey, it's a good idea to take some drinks, healthy snacks and sandwiches, particularly if you're not going to stop and have a meal somewhere.

Problems with Eating

Dislike of Specific Foods

It's quite common for children to dislike foods with a strong taste such as leeks, Brussels sprouts, onions, some fruits and salad vegetables. Most children don't like lettuce until they are older. It's also common for children to dislike fish or eggs, or to prefer fruit to vegetables. Some children cannot tolerate eggs until they are around five years of age. Many children don't like certain textures of food and will spit food out if it is lumpy or has a tough skin. When you stop pureeing food and start to give it to your baby with 'bits' in it, you may well find he spits the bits out. Try mashing it with a fork and gradually introducing it in a more lumpy form; you don't want him to stop eating it because of the lumps and as he gets bigger he will get used to it.

If your child has a definite dislike and is otherwise eating well, I would advise you not to offer that food for a while but to go back and try it again after a few weeks. It's not worth making an issue out of it. If you really want your child to eat a particular food, you could try mixing it with potato or disguising it in a sauce. Many children won't eat a separate portion of green vegetables but will happily eat them mixed into a pasta sauce.

Going off Food

'My daughter was a wonderful eater to start with and ate every single vegetable from leeks to parsnip to broccoli. Now, at two years, she will only eat vegetables if they are disguised in a casserole or bolognese sauce.'

Mother of two

Nearly all children during the second year of their lives will go off food at some point. This is perfectly normal. It can be a shock to you as parents when your child has eaten everything you have put in front of him and then suddenly for no apparent reason he doesn't want to know. He may become fussy and not eat everything you have been giving him, or he may completely go off his food. Take heart; you are not alone, and you can work through it and your child will be a good eater again. Most children grow into adults who enjoy their food and have a healthy appetite and are none the worse for going through this stage of not eating.

If your child is ill with a fever or a stomach upset then she probably will not want to eat at all. Don't push her to eat; just ensure that she is having plenty to drink. You will find, though, that she takes several days after she has recovered to regain her appetite and in fact may fuss over her food for some weeks to come. When she is teething, too, she will probably have days when she doesn't want to eat. Many children don't like a spoon in their mouth when they are teething and for a few days they will often go off food that has to be chewed. If she has had a period of illness, be patient with her as her appetite returns, and you will probably find that after a while she can't get enough to eat!

Another reason for a child not eating is an upset or change in family life. One of my daughters was two years old when my husband went into hospital for an operation. She refused to eat all the time he was away, and then when he came home she gradually started to eat again. If there is a new baby in the family and you are busy with it, it is very likely that your toddler will go off his food. Any family trauma can cause a young child to stop eating, so be sensitive to his needs if this is the case.

This is also the age when your child is beginning to assert her independence and trying out new behaviour patterns. Toddlers and young children get engrossed in play and sometimes can't be bothered to come to the table to eat – there are much more exciting things to do! Also there is a slowdown in her growth so her appetite may not be as great. You will be very fortunate to go through the toddler years without your child going off her food at some point; remember that some children go off food for no reason other than just being a toddler. Also remember that your child is not rejecting you when she doesn't eat and is not doing it to upset you.

What do you do when your toddler won't eat? First, don't fill him up with snacks between meals. As breakfast is usually the best meal of the day, if your child is not eating well, include plenty of healthy food here and let him have a good amount. One of my clients told me that she has found it very helpful to think about her daughter having a balanced diet over the course of a week rather than worrying about what she eats every day. Eat together at the table when possible and not in front of the television or other distractions, so that you are as relaxed as possible.

One of the most important things is to try not to make an issue about eating. I think there are two ways of dealing with your child refusing what you are giving her to eat. The first option is to tell her a story to take her mind off eating, making sure you are sitting down at the table with her and giving her your attention while you continue to feed her. Often this tactic will work, especially with a child who has had a good appetite. I have told endless stories out of my head while I've sat and fed a child who didn't want to eat, and it *very* often works. The other option is to take the food away when she refuses, even if she has only had a few mouthfuls. When our children were growing up, if they didn't eat I would take away the food and they would have to get down from the table and wait until the next meal. Usually by the next meal they were very hungry and would eat a good amount. If you prefer, you can give her her dessert and then allow her down from the table without making any fuss about it. However, what you don't want is for your child to learn that she can refuse her first course and go straight to dessert all the time. Whichever option you choose, try to just give small amounts so that she is not overwhelmed.

There are some children who have always had problems with eating for whatever reason, and often this goes back to when they were babies and may have had feeding problems or were in special care. I have found also that children who have sleep problems are usually bad eaters too; these two things nearly always seem to go together. If this is the case with your child and you are not dealing with a toddler who has gone off his food for the usual reasons, then I would suggest you get some professional help. Please be reassured that you are not the only parents to experience this, and with the right treatment your child is very likely to have a good appetite in time.

Not Eating Enough

It's easy to worry that your toddler is not having enough to eat during the day, especially if she's been a good eater during the first year of life. In fact, most children's appetites decrease quite dramatically for a while during the toddler years and in spite of this they continue to grow and develop quite normally, so don't worry if you find this happens with your child. You may also find that your child is too tired to have her main meal at teatime; if this is the case then give her her bigger meal at lunchtime. You may need to do this for a while, particularly if she is changing her daytime sleep habits. One mistake it's easy to make is to let your child have lots of snacks between meals, which then fills her up so that she eats very little at mealtimes. If you are giving your toddler bottles of milk throughout the day, this can also fill her up so that she doesn't have an appetite for meals.

If your child has serious eating problems or you are having battles over mealtimes and everyone is getting very upset, this can lead to a vicious circle where you get stressed too. As parents, it's quite natural to want to provide and make sure that our children have plenty to eat during the day, and if this is not happening it can make us feel very anxious and worried. If you are struggling with this, talk to your health visitor or general practitioner.

Mess

When your toddler starts to feed himself there is going to be some mess, as this is all part of him experimenting with his spoon and cup. He will discover that he can blow bubbles and will play to the gallery, and it can be very funny when he is doing this and learning to feed himself. I believe, though, that children need not be allowed to throw their food round the kitchen or make a terrible mess by smearing it into their hair or tipping food all over themselves. You can gently teach your child that this is not acceptable, and he will quickly learn, especially if you don't let him get into a habit of playing with his food. I am not saying that you shouldn't have any fun at mealtimes, but you need to decide what amount of mess is acceptable to you and set your boundaries.

It's a good idea to have a plastic sheet under her high chair or chair, as this makes it much easier to collect the bits of food that get dropped. You could also use a plate with a suction cup that sticks to the tray or table, as for a while she will not be able to get this off. As she gets bigger and sits at the table to have her meals, it is a good idea to start teaching some table manners such as not throwing food or spilling drinks so that she knows how to behave when you take her out or she goes to friends' houses. If you as parents don't teach table manners then nobody else will!

Weaning off the Breast or Bottle

Why Wean?

Many mothers ask me why they should wean their baby off the breast or bottle – won't the baby just do it naturally? Unfortunately the longer you go on feeding from the breast or bottle the harder it becomes to wean your child, as he gets more and more attached to it and it becomes a habit. He will also be having too much milk, which fills him up and leaves no room for food, and you could then find you have a toddler who doesn't want to eat. Nutritionally your child needs much more than milk can offer as he becomes a toddler, so for his general growth and development he needs food as well as some milk. He no longer needs the sucking action that he needed as a baby to help his jaw develop; instead he needs the chewing action to help him in his speech development. Long-term use of a bottle with a constant flow of liquid from the teat can damage his teeth as they are growing and coming through. This happens particularly if you give him a bottle of juice to walk about with throughout the day.

Another reason for weaning is that most mothers don't want a toddler pulling up their shirt for a breast-feed at any moment. It is also part of your child's ability to become independent, and she needs to be able to drink from a cup for social reasons too. If she is going into a preschool or nursery it will be better for her if she is weaned before she is running around with older children who do not have a bottle.

When Should I Wean?

When should you wean your baby or toddler, and is there a right time to do it? First of all, whether you are breast-feeding or bottle-feeding, you must feel ready yourself to wean. I think a good time to do it is when your child is about one year old, though of course this can be flexible by a month or so either side. By this age, whether he is breast- or bottle-fed, he should be drinking well from a cup. You may have breast-fed for six months and then put your baby on a bottle, so to wean him off the bottle at about a year may feel right for you. If you are still breast-feeding you may feel it is going to be a wrench to stop. You need to think about it and talk to your partner so that you feel it is the right time to do it. It is easier to wean at one year than it is by the age of two, as your child will be much more aware of everything by then and you will find it more of a battle. I would strongly advise that you think seriously about weaning from about one year onwards.

If you are having another baby, then I would suggest you wean your toddler off the breast before the baby comes, although I have known mothers who have fed their two-year-old up to the birth of their next baby and then stopped feeding her when the baby arrived. Don't try to wean if your child is unwell, as she will only want milk and will be distressed if you take the bottle away or stop breast-feeding.

How Do I Wean My Toddler off the Bottle?

The thought of weaning can be rather stressful, but there are ways that we can do it. We'll look at cutting out your child's bottle first. I believe there are two ways that you can do this, and you need to decide which will suit you better. You can use the 'cold turkey' method, which is to take all bottles away at the same time. I feel this is too sudden for most children and it is much kinder to do it gently, either by reducing the amount of milk you put in the bottle so after a few days there is nothing or by taking away daytime feeds first and then dealing with the early morning and evening feeds after that.

There are several things to remember when you are weaning your child off the bottle. He is likely to be unsettled for a few days so make sure that you give him lots of cuddles and that he has his cuddly blanket or toy when he goes into his cot or bed. Depending on the age of your child, you may well find he has tantrums when he is tired and wanting a bottle for comfort. This is the time, of course, to put him on your lap and cuddle him up to you, telling him that you love him but that the bottles have all gone away. Don't let him get overtired, as this will exacerbate the situation. Don't let your child walk around with an empty bottle to suck when he wants to, as this will not help him to drop using the bottle. If he has been used to going to the fridge and getting his bottle out, don't let him do this; offer a drink from his cup instead. Once he has had enough to drink don't let him run around with the cup but take it away.

Weaning from Bottle to Cup

This is the method that I use and I find it works well. First, it is a good idea to have a new cup for her drinks. It is amazing how children become attached to their cup or plate very quickly, and this helps with the transition from bottle to cup. The first step is to replace the daytime bottles with a cup of water or juice (by daytime I mean breakfast, lunch and teatime). This probably leaves you with an early morning bottle and another one just before she goes to bed at night.

If he has been used to having a bottle on and off all day, be firm and determined that you are not going to give in. Take him out for a walk or distract his attention in some way at the time when he would normally have a bottle. You will find this works quite quickly, as his mind is on other things. If he has been used to having a bottle for daytime sleeps, again, take him out in the buggy and let him have his cuddly toy or muslin. You may have to do this for a few days until he has forgotten about his bottle. Then let him have his nap in his cot once you have established that he will sleep without his bottle. Make up your mind that you are not going to give in, as he doesn't need it. You will be pleased when you have persevered and he no longer asks for his bottle. This process normally only takes a few days.

Once you have established drinking from a cup during the day, move to the early morning bottle when she wakes. As we talked about in Chapter 4, try not to go in to her if she wakes early for a bottle, but let her play in her cot for a while. Then get her dressed and give her breakfast with a good cup of milk to drink. Don't worry if breakfast is a little earlier for a few days; you will probably find that she eats a very good breakfast. If she has cereal you can measure the amount of milk you pour on her cereal if you are concerned that she is not going to have enough, and you may be surprised how much it is. Don't worry that she will be missing out on her milk, as she will make this up in the foods she has during the day that have calcium in them. If she is having a balanced diet she does not need the same volume of milk anyway.

The last bottle of the day to drop is the bedtime one. When he has his tea at around 5 p.m. offer him milk in a cup, and do this for several days before you stop the bottle. This way he will be quite full with his supper and milk and will not be hungry for a bottle at bedtime. Bath him and then offer him a little drink of milk in his cup when you put him to bed. He may not want this at all and be happy to settle without his bottle. If he is around a year old he probably won't make a fuss at all, but if he is older he may, as his bottle is all part of the bedtime routine. If he is old enough for you to explain what you are doing then I recommend this; you can even make a story up about why he doesn't need a bottle and where they are going to go. The other way to cut his bedtime feed out is to reduce the amount of milk he has in his bottle every night until he is having so little that it is not worth having it in a bottle.

How do you deal with a child who wakes hungry in the night and wants a bottle? Make sure that your toddler has had enough to eat and drink at teatime. As your child gets older and maybe has a fairly energetic play time after tea (this could be in the summer when the weather is good and she plays outside), she may well need something else to eat before she goes to bed. I think a bowl of cereal, a banana or a piece of toast and a cup of milk is a good way to fill her up, and she should not wake hungry in the night for a drink. Make sure she brushes her teeth after she has had something to eat and drink. If your child does wake in the night and has been used to having a bottle, then once you've decided to wean I would advise you not to give a bottle to pacify her but a drink in a cup instead.

Older Toddlers

I know one little girl who was still having bottles in the day and at night when she was three years old. Her parents asked me to get her off them while they were away for a few days. I talked about it with the little girl and told her that she was a big girl and didn't need her bottles any more, and that she could stand at the sink and wash them all up and we would put them in a box for another baby. She thought this was a great idea and dutifully washed them all and put them in a box. It was quite easy to stop the daytime bottles as she soon was eating well and didn't want the milk. She settled well at bedtime after a few days without a bottle, and woke in the night once, but settled down to sleep again after having a cuddle with me. When her mother came home she wanted the bottle again, as she associated Mummy with bottles. Mummy was firm and didn't give in, and after about a week she had forgotten about her bottles and never looked back. You have to be very firm and determined if your child is this age, though.

Stopping Breast-feeding

Stopping breast-feeding, like bottle-feeding, has to be your decision and can be quite an emotional time for you. On the other hand, you may well feel you have done it for long enough and just want your body back. Either way is perfectly normal, and it is up to you when you do it. A lot of women go on giving a breast-feed just at bedtime and feel loath to give this up. When you do stop you are likely to feel hormonal and emotional, but this is quite normal. You will be surprised how good you feel when your milk has dried up and it is possible that you will have more energy too.

As with bottle-feeding, I feel it is a good idea to start thinking about weaning your child off the breast when he is about one year old. As he goes into his second year he will become more attached to you, and it is better to begin to separate this exclusive relationship you have with him, for several reasons. It is an opportunity for him to form a greater bond with his dad, and you will be sharing more of the parenting together. It also means that someone other than you and your partner can feed him and settle him. It helps him to begin to become independent from you, as this is one of the skills we teach our children as they grow up.

Weaning from Breast to Cup

If you are still breast-feeding through the day then I would stop these feeds first. The lunchtime one can be the first one to drop, and she probably won't notice it if she is having a good mixed diet. Replace her milk feed with water or juice to drink. Also cut out her daytime feeds or snacks if you give any to settle her for her naps. The sooner you do this the better, as it is more difficult to drop these snacks as she gets into her second year. She is getting bigger and they can become a real habit, and you may find she throws tantrums. Take her out in her buggy to have her daytime naps for a few days until she forgets about suckling to go to sleep. Once this is established, put her in her cot for her nap without a breast-feed. Give a drink of milk if you wish but do this in her high chair so that it is different from having a feed from you.

Once you have sorted the daytime feeds out then drop the early morning breast-feed if you are still doing this. If he is waking very early, go in to him and settle him back down, maybe with a little drink from a cup, then get him up when you are ready to give him his breakfast. Do not give a breast-feed but give him his cereal and whatever else he has for breakfast, giving him his milk in a cup halfway through his breakfast. You will probably find that he is very happy with this and doesn't miss this feed at all.

The last feed to stop is the one at bedtime, which is of course often a comfort feed. You can do this by decreasing the amount she suckles each night, or by just deciding to stop on a certain night. Her reaction to this will probably depend on her age and how much breast-feeding she has been having. Toddlers will often want to suck for comfort when they are tired, so it is a good idea to make sure she has had plenty to drink at teatime and to have a good wind-down time before bed, making sure she is not overtired. It is a good idea for Daddy or someone whom she knows well to put her to bed rather than Mummy, to avoid reminding her of breast-feeding. Do this for several nights and she will soon forget about feeding to settle. You could well prepare for this by getting Daddy to settle her even when you are still breast-feeding, if he doesn't normally do bedtime. You may find your toddler adapts to this quickly. If she doesn't settle easily without a breast-feed at first, persevere, as you will find that she does after a few days.

What if you've been feeding him to settle him in the night if he hasn't got a good sleeping pattern going? You must be sure in yourself that you are not going to give a feed, as this in itself is half the battle. If he wakes for whatever reason and you feel he needs a drink, just give water out of a cup. Again, do persevere, as it really will pay off and you will find you have weaned him without any trauma.

What Should My Toddler Drink?

It is perfectly all right to give your toddler full-fat cow's milk from the age of twelve months, unless she has a dairy or lactose intolerance. If she has, then you need to see your general practitioner and get advice on what you should give to replace milk. If your child does not like the taste of cow's milk because she has been on formula, then I suggest you dilute the formula with some cow's milk, doing it gradually over a few days. She will soon take to the new taste and be happy with cow's milk.

Daytime drinks can be water or diluted fruit juice. Some parents do not want their children to have fruit juice as they worry that it will be bad for their teeth; however, it is only bad if they have it in a bottle and continually suck it as they walk around or sit in their cot or in the car, so that there is a continual flow of juice going into their mouths. I think it is a good idea for young children to have some fruit juice in their diets, as it is full of vitamin C and it is good for them to have a variety of tastes to drink. Both fruit juice and water help to keep your toddler's skin healthy and are good for preventing constipation. You can also give pureed fruit mixed with yoghurt and milk as a smoothie or just a plain milkshake with fruit in it. It is not a good idea to give fizzy drinks, as this doesn't do children's teeth any good at all. Do not give your young child coffee, and certainly not alcohol. Some children drink tea at an early age; I would give a good decaffeinated tea or rooibos (redbush), which is a naturally caffeine-free type of tea.

Closing Thoughts

Eating and weaning off the breast or bottle are undoubtedly two of the main challenges of the toddler years. My hope is that this chapter has taken some of the mystery out of this and that you are able to persevere through the tricky times. By the school years, most children are not battling over food so often and will really enjoy family mealtimes, especially if they've been encouraged as toddlers.

CHAPTER 6

Potty Training

Potty training seems to have become a big issue for many families today and I often wonder why this has happened. When I did my nursing training we put babies on potties from a very early age; of course this was not 'formal' potty training, as a young baby has no idea at all of bowel control. After the baby had his feed I would put him on a potty on my lap, holding him with both hands, and more often than not he would perform. This of course was to save a dirty nappy, not to train the baby. When I had my own children I did the same with them, although not at every feed. I am not suggesting that this is what you have to do, but I wonder, looking back, if it enabled young children to get used to a potty when they were very young so that it was part of everyday life. Today, children are often not shown a potty until they are much older, and it can then become an issue.

I don't remember having any problems with moving on to potty-training our children, as it was all part of the daily routine. As I have been writing this chapter I have talked to many friends who brought up their children in the 1970s, and a large proportion of them said they also put their babies on a potty from an early age and that training in general wasn't a problem, as it was all part of everyday life. I wonder if some of the problems today arise because many women are back at work and so don't have quite the same opportunities as we did to be consistent with potty-training. Equally, women at home with their children tend to have a much fuller social life nowadays and may not spend as much time at home, making it rather more difficult to teach their child to use a potty. I also believe training can become an issue nowadays as it is often left so late, and then there is a sense of urgency about getting it right very quickly. If children are going off to preschool or nursery then they are often expected to be clean and dry, and it can be a big worry for you as parents if you haven't managed to achieve this.

Reasons for Potty Training

Whenever you decide to start potty training, try to remember that for your child it is all part of normal development to become dry and clean, just like learning to walk, talk, get dressed and feed herself. Also, of course, it is a social expectation, and rightly so. You don't want your child to be wet or have soiled pants as she grows up and it will be your desire as parents to make sure that she learns to be clean and dry like her friends. Part of toilet training is helping children to learn personal hygiene, such as washing their hands, which in time of course they will do for themselves. Most nurseries and preschools will want your child to be clean and dry when they come for the day. Day nurseries, however, usually take much younger children so will be set up for nappy-changing. Of course, all children have accidents and the nursery should understand and be able to deal with it without any problem.

When Should I Start?

There are many different schools of thought as to when you should start to potty-train your child, and some people can become quite heated over it and have very strong views. There is the view that you shouldn't start till your child is around three years of age, but personally I feel that is leaving it too long, as most children are ready well before this. I would certainly have a potty for your child from quite a young age and keep it in the bathroom, so that he gets used to it being there. The idea is to make it all as normal as possible and to introduce it as part of his bathtime routine, just as much as cleaning his teeth or washing his hair. My experience with potty training is that once your child can walk properly and sit unaided without toppling over, there is no reason why you shouldn't start. I would start by making it very natural: show him his potty when you undress him for his bath at night and sit him on it or let him stand to do a 'pee-pee'. He will very soon make the connection between the potty and doing a wee or a poo.

I would make a start some time between when your child is eighteen months and two years of age. I don't believe there is a 'magic' time to start. Remember that children are all different and some will be ready before others. In my experience little girls seem to take to it quicker than little boys and are often ready earlier too. So if you make a start and you don't seem to be making any progress, leave it for a while and start again in a few weeks' time. Don't feel guilty if this happens, as it is nothing to do with your child's intelligence, whether she was a late walker or talker, or whether you are going about it in the right way or not. Don't feel pressured to start potty training just because friends are starting. A good sign of a child being ready to start is if you find she has a dry nappy for quite a while in the day or if she wakes up from her daytime nap with a dry nappy, as this shows that she is starting to have some bladder control.

A sensible time to start is when everything at home is going smoothly and you are not just about to go away on holiday or start working. It is a good idea to choose a time when you are going to be around and haven't got too much to do, so that you can really concentrate on it for a few days. I have known mothers who made sure they could stay near to home for the first few days, just to make it easier all round. If your child has a nanny, childminder or grandparent looking after them, let them know how you are potty training so you can all be consistent. Don't start potty training when you are just about to have a new baby, or if your child has been ill, or there is some major change happening within the family. A house move can be a major event for a child as well as for you, so don't try to start to potty-train if you are just about to move. Make sure that you as parents are ready to start and to give it a try. And remember that *all* children in time become clean and dry. It is sensible to start potty training when all is as calm as possible on the home front.

Equipment

When shopping for a potty make sure you get a sturdy one. A potty that sits firmly on the floor will feel safer for a child to sit on than one that tips over easily. You may find it helpful to have more than one potty, depending on how many bathrooms you have. If your child is of an age when he can understand, you can take him to the shop to buy his special potty so that you make it rather exciting to use. However, it's not necessary to buy a novelty potty that sings or lights up! You can also get a travel potty with disposable liners if you need to do a lot of travelling. If you have a little boy, you need to sit him on the potty with the highest part of the potty in front of him, and little girls can sit either way round. My eldest daughter has a potty chair, which is a solid frame with a potty in the middle that lifts out for emptying, and her children have used this for quite some time.

Trainer seats for the toilet need to fit well. If they don't and your child feels as if she is going to fall off or fall into the toilet, this will not help her to feel safe, and you will find that she soon doesn't want to sit on the toilet. If your child does want to use the toilet, then get a good seat that will clip onto the top of it, or you can buy a combined seat with a child-sized seat that folds up out of the way when you don't need it. I would also get a plastic step to put in front of the toilet so that she can climb up and get on herself as she gets more used to using it. If you have a little boy teach him to lift the toilet seat, stand in front of it (once he's tall enough) and aim down into the bowl, otherwise you will constantly have wee all over the back of the toilet. Some little boys think this is rather a good game!

Pull-up disposable trainer pants are a good idea, as your child can feel very grown-up because he can stand up to put them on. Make sure they are not too tight and are easy to get off quickly. As he becomes better at bladder control, change to cotton pants. He will feel more uncomfortable when wet or dirty in these than in disposables, and this will help him to want to be dry. Make sure his clothes are easy to undo and you are not grappling with a zip fastener or buttons when he wants to wee. If this happens you are bound to have an accident, as speed is the essence when training. Towelling pants are comfortable and wash and dry easily. Also buy a good plastic sheet for the bed for when you take him out of nappies at night. I would recommend getting a fitted plastic sheet that covers the whole mattress, as tie-on sheets can move too easily, and you can end up with a wet bed.

How Do I Potty-train?

Getting Your Child Familiar with a Potty

Before you start potty training you can let your child come into the toilet with you when you do a wee, if you feel comfortable with this. In my experience this is one of the best ways to get a child interested in using a potty or the toilet. I did it with my own children and even do it with my grandchildren. You will be amazed at how quickly a child can learn from this, very soon putting the two together, and feeling very grown-up when she actually does a wee on the potty in the bathroom – just like Mummy!

When you talk to your child about going to the loo, it is helpful to decide what you are going to call passing urine and bowel movements. I think it is important that you have names, such as 'penny', 'wee', 'poo', 'poop' and so on, that you feel happy for both your child and you to use. Lots of families have their own names for these, so use whatever you feel comfortable with. When our children were growing up the girls had a doll that drank water and then wet itself, and they were fascinated with this. I am not sure if it helped them to be potty-trained but it did make the business of talking about weeing much more natural and playful. Some parents use this 'play' approach by putting a doll or a teddy on the potty first, to encourage their child to sit on it after teddy has been.

Most children have a regular time when they will have a bowel movement, so watch out for this time and put him on the potty in anticipation. Quite often, this time is just after breakfast and/or lunch. Often your child will dash off to a corner to do a poo in his nappy behind a sofa or a chair when he is becoming aware of having a bowel movement, and he may also say 'poo' or point to his nappy. If you catch him in time to put him on the potty, give him lots of praise for being so grown-up, let him help you empty the potty down the toilet, flush the toilet and then wash his hands (see Chapter 9 for more on hand-washing).

Helpful hints

- *Let your child come into the toilet with you.*
- *Talk openly about wees and poos – in your own words!*
- *Put your child on the potty when she normally does a poo.*
- *Give lots of praise if she performs; don't make a big deal if she doesn't.*
- *Keep her in nappies at this point.*
- *Make sure you wash both your own and your child's hands.*

Daytime Potty Training

When you have decided to start potty training in earnest, I think it is a good idea to make it part of the daily routine that your child will come to expect. When you get your child up in the morning or get him dressed, this is a good time to take his nappy off and sit him on his potty or the toilet. You may not always catch him in time, and he may wake because he has done a poo in his nappy and needs changing. Most people use a potty, but you may prefer to go straight to a trainer seat on the toilet. Make sure he is feeling secure and can't slip, and give him books and toys to play with to keep him sitting down. If he is on his potty this should be easy to do; if he is on the toilet you may need to put a chair next to it and put some books and toys on that.

Try not to hover over her. Give her space to sit there and feel comfortable, and with luck she will perform for you. If she starts wriggling and wants to get off, try distracting her by reading a favourite story to her. If she is happy sitting there you can always go and do some chores nearby, but keep an eye on her in case she suddenly gets up and walks away. If she does a wee or a poo, praise her and let her help you tip it down the toilet. This will help her to feel grown-up and that she is doing well. Wipe your child's bottom after she's done a wee or a poo, always wiping from front to back for little girls, as it's more common for them to get urinary tract infections. You can teach your child to wipe her bottom, but most children under three will not be able to wipe themselves properly. Once you've finished, wash both your own and your child's hands. If nothing happens after about five minutes, you could try turning the cold tap on in the basin to encourage her to do a wee. However, if she still hasn't done anything, don't worry. Just put the potty away and move on and do whatever you were going to do next.

To start with I usually wouldn't put him on the potty again till after lunch, when you then do exactly the same as you did after breakfast. Then when you come to bathtime take his nappy and clothes off and put him on the potty again. Again praise him if he has performed, but don't be cross or angry if he hasn't. Let him run round without his nappy on for a little while when he comes out of the bath; just make sure he can't do a wee on your best carpet! I know one little boy who will do a wee each time before he has his bath, and he likes to stand up to do it, 'just like Daddy'. He will then help empty it down the toilet, and even though he is only twenty months old he understands quite well what he is doing. Once your child has this kind of awareness, it is a great time to start potty training seriously.

When your child has got used to the routine of using the potty at breakfast, lunch and bathtime I would start putting her on her potty during the morning and again during the afternoon at about 45-minute intervals, especially if she has had something to drink. What you're aiming to do is to help your child to be dry by anticipating when she might need a wee, rather than waiting for her to tell you – which might be too late. You will usually find that a child will be clean (able to poo in a potty) before she is dry, but sometimes the two go together. If you start training in the summer it is easier, particularly if you have a garden. Your child can run around in the garden with a pair of pants on and it is quick and easy to catch her to put her on the potty if she suddenly starts to do a wee. Also if it is warm she can run around without any pants on, so if accidents happen it doesn't matter.

It's a good idea to continue to use a nappy or pull-ups when your child naps in the daytime, as often he will wee as soon as he wakes up, and then you have a wet cot. If his nappy is dry when you get him up then put him on the potty before you put his nappy or pants on. It's also useful to use a nappy or pull-ups when you go on a journey until you're absolutely sure that your child will let you know when he needs to go.

You can use rewards, such as stickers on a chart, sweets or visits to a favourite place, to encourage your child to use her potty. I wouldn't use this method initially, though, but keep it for when your child is old enough to know what she is doing and if you don't seem to be making any headway. As she learns to use her potty then phase the rewards out gently. One of my clients gave her children a sweet each time they used the potty, but this only worked as her children rarely had sweets at other times. Finally, persevere and don't give up. Remember that you are bound to have accidents for quite some time to come. Most children of three years and over will still have occasional accidents, so be patient. Be sensitive to your child's feelings and don't make a fuss about accidents in front of other people, as this can really make an issue of toilet training.

Helpful hints

- Put your child on the potty in the morning, after meals and at bathtime.
- Move on to trying the potty at roughly 45-minute intervals during the day.
- Be aware when your child might need a wee, especially after drinks.
- Use towelling or cotton pants during the daytime (as your child will feel when he is wet in these).
- Use a nappy or pull-ups at night-time and nap times.
- Your child will often be clean first, then dry.
- Persevere calmly – accidents will happen!

Going Out When Potty Training

When out and about during the day, it's a good idea to take your child to different toilets so she gets used to weeing in other places, even if you use your own potty or travel potty. Try to find out where the toilet is before your child is ready to go, as speed is of the essence! Always take plenty of clean pants or pull-ups and a clean set of clothes, as well as baby wipes. If your child needs to wee when you're out for a walk, it's a good idea to give her some privacy and not encourage her to perform in front of everyone. It is of course easier for little boys, and for little girls you need to lift them up with their back to you and help them to squat to do a wee while you hold them. As girls get older they can do this themselves. Unfortunately, it often happens that as soon as you're in the middle of nowhere your child wants to do a poo. Find a quiet place away from everyone and hold her so that she can squat to do it. Remember to take baby wipes or tissues with you to wipe her bottom.

If you are going on a journey, I would put your child in pull-ups or a nappy while you are travelling. If your child sleeps on the journey, he will probably do a wee as soon as he wakes up, and you don't want to arrive at your destination with a wet child and a wet car. Remember to take plenty of spare wipes, pants, pull-ups or nappies and spare sets of clothes when you go away for a few days. The disposable pull-up pants are useful when travelling, especially if you don't want to have to do lots of washing while you are away. Remember to take the potty or toilet seat with you if you go away for a night or so. You may find that having his own potty will make all the difference to keeping the potty training going while you are away. If your child gets upset and doesn't want to use the potty or toilet while you are away, and you have only just started training him, then I wouldn't persist but leave it till you get home again.

Potty Training with Older Children

Don't despair if you have an older toddler and you haven't done anything about potty training yet. An older child will have a greater awareness of when she is wet or dirty and is often concerned about having clean hands and not wanting a dirty nappy on. You can use quite a direct approach with an older child, as she will usually understand more and respond quite quickly. Several years ago, I was looking after a family of children while the parents went on holiday. The three-year-old was not clean or dry and the mother asked me if I could get her out of nappies while I was there. We took her nappies away and said that she was going to be very grown-up like her older siblings and we weren't going to have nappies any more. I started putting her on the potty after breakfast and on and off during the day, and within two weeks she was clean and dry during the day. We made a game of it and said how pleased Mummy was going to be when she came back from her holiday. At three she was old enough to understand. We would even go out to the shops without a nappy on and then find a toilet when she needed one. It didn't take her very long to know when she wanted to do a wee and she would tell me. After two weeks I took her nappies away at night and within three weeks she became dry and clean at night too. So it can be done! Remember, though, that this little girl was three years old and had older siblings to look up to. Also some children are easier to train than others.

Working Towards Being Dry at Night

The most important thing to focus on in the toddler years is helping your child to be dry and clean during the day. In fact, few children are dry at night by the time they are three. However, you can start to get your child ready to be dry at night as he approaches the age of three. Some older toddlers will want to have their nappy off at night, especially once they are dry during the day. The two main pieces of advice I give to parents starting to get their child out of nappies at night are to cut down on drinks after 6 p.m. and to lift him and put him on his potty between 10 and 11 p.m. Don't cut down on your child's fluids if he is ill, and if he is really thirsty let him have sips but try not to let him have too much. Some parents I've spoken to have been worried about waking children in the late evening to go on the potty; however, in my experience they always do a wee and usually don't fully wake up, so you can put them straight back to sleep. If your child is wet night after night once you've tried these methods, he is probably not ready yet, so take a month off and then try again, as there's no hurry.

Problems with Potty Training

The main thing to remember if you are having problems with potty training is not to let it become a battleground between you and your child. If you have heated arguments about potty training, this only makes matters worse. If you are feeling cross with your child that she's not progressing, try not to let her see this, as she can end up feeling more negative about using the potty. It's much better for both of you to take some time out, go back to nappies or trainer pants, put the potty away and come back to it in a few weeks' time. I have known children who decide they want to be grown-up and go straight to using the toilet once their parents have taken this approach. Another approach is to sit your child on the potty while she's engrossed in something completely different, for example watching the television, just to distract her.

Taking a Long Time to Be Clean and Dry

Patience is important with potty training, especially if it is taking longer than you had reckoned on. Usually boys will take longer to get the hang of potty training than girls. If your child is physically and emotionally well, and it's taking time to get him clean and dry, he may just be a late developer. Lateness in becoming dry can run in families, so check this if you are concerned, and you may find one of your own family took time becoming dry. The main thing to remember is that it will happen; try not to worry about it, and all of a sudden your child will be dry and you will be thrilled that you have come through this stage. Always remember that there will be times when your child has an accident; this doesn't mean you have to start all over again. If you're not making any headway at all with potty training by the time your child is three, then I would advise that you talk to your doctor or health visitor.

Accidents and 'Holding On'

Many potty-trained children will wee in their pants if they are nervous, excited or frightened, so don't be surprised if this happens. It's also very common for children to wet themselves if they are engrossed in what they are doing and forget to go to the toilet, or if they are too shy to go to the toilet at preschool or nursery. On the other hand, some children will hold on to their wee because they don't want to use a toilet in a strange place, although this usually won't happen with a child under three. If your child holds on and on to wee, put her in a warm bath, which will enable her to relax and do a wee.

Some children will be weeing in a potty but will only poo in their nappy or pants. If your child is doing this, be patient and try not to make a fuss about it, as he will in time use his potty. Some children will go for days without doing a poo, and this can be a worry to parents if they do it on a regular basis. 'Holding on' to poo is more common than we think, because it is not talked about. This may happen for all sorts of reasons; perhaps upset within the family home, or the arrival of a new baby. Try to remember that your child is not doing this deliberately. He may just be anxious about doing a poo, particularly if it has been painful at any time, for example due to constipation. In the first instance, make sure your child has plenty of fruit, vegetables and fibre and lots to drink. If this problem continues you may need to get medical advice. Some children hold on to poo as a reaction to stress in their lives, and if this is the case you need to find somebody who you can talk about this with. I was talking to a young woman recently whose child had held on to poo, and did this for quite some time. It happened when her father left the family home and she was going through a traumatic time. Obviously the child was feeling upset and insecure and this was how she reacted. In time, and with medical help, this problem did resolve.

Illnesses

Little girls can often get urinary tract infections, which make it very painful to wee, and you will find that they are continually wet. If your child has an infection, see your doctor for some antibiotics and put her back in pull-ups until she has recovered. If your child has diarrhoea, it is better to put him back in nappies until he is well again. It is not fair on him or the family for him to have constant accidents while he is not well. It is quite normal for a child not to do a poo each day, so don't worry that he is constipated unless he is straining to go and produces a movement like rabbit droppings. If your child is constipated, first make sure his diet has plenty of fruit, vegetables and fibre. You can give him prune juice or syrup of figs to drink. Never give any stronger laxatives to your child unless under medical advice.

Life Changes

If your toddler is potty-trained, you may find that she regresses when a new baby arrives in the family, and she may wet or soil her pants for a few weeks. I would advise that you make as little fuss as possible, and just put her back in nappies or pull-ups for a while until she has adjusted to this change in her life. Starting nursery or preschool can also make your child very nervous, and she may seem to go backwards with her potty training. Any significant family change is likely to have an effect on potty training, but your child will get back on track.

Things Not to Worry About

Don't worry...

- *if your child takes longer than you'd hoped to get the hang of potty training.*
- *if he has a relapse, especially if he is ill or if you have a new baby.*
- *if your child has potty-training accidents.*
- *if your child jumps off the potty and wees all over the floor – it happens!*
- *if he wants to just sit and play with his toys on his potty.*
- *if your children take different amounts of time to be clean and dry (it's often easier to train younger children as they can copy their older brothers or sisters).*

CHAPTER 7

Play

Play is very important for children of all ages and in the toddler years it is all about learning, helping your child to make sense of the world and most of all having great fun! It's easy to underestimate the effect that play has on your child, but it really is a vital part of her development. When you watch a child play, what she does can sometimes seem pointless from an adult point of view, but it is important for your child just to explore and have fun, as well as doing activities that seem to have more of an 'educational' value. Toddler groups and play dates are invaluable at this stage for your child to learn to play with others.

There will be a massive development in the complexity of your child's play and his ability to play and co-operate with others over the years from one to three. During the toddler years, your child will play much more with other children both of his own age and older. In general, at about eighteen months your child will start to take more notice of others his age and may copy what another child is doing, although he probably will play better with an older child. He may not be good at sharing at this age and may fight with other children his age quite a lot over toys. Between two and three your child will play together with others much more co-operatively, and by the end of this time he may play quite long, involved make-believe games.

Your child also needs time to play on her own so that as she grows up she can entertain herself. You will notice that as she gets older she will make up imaginary games and will probably play quite happily in her own world for a while. It is very important that you as parents also spend time playing with her, as she still needs your direction and help in the toddler years. When you spend time getting involved in her games it makes her feel loved and secure, as she has her favourite thing: your time and attention. Always remember that play activities should first and foremost be enjoyable for both you and your child. Children can be overwhelmed if they have too many toys to play with at the same time. It is a good idea to have a change of toys every now and again. Keep some toys in the cupboard and bring them out when she gets bored of what is in her toy box. This varies things for her and helps to keep her play fresh.

Other useful aids to play are music and singing, which are an important part of a child's development. Most children seem to have a natural response to music from a very early age, and the rhythm of music and singing can help children with speech development. Children who are upset will often calm down when they hear music or singing, and become peaceful. You will soon notice if your child is going to be musical, and if this is so, do encourage him by playing CDs, having the radio on, or if you play a musical instrument, playing it to him, and of course singing to him too. Children get a lot of pleasure from singing and dancing as they are learning to perform, and this teaches them confidence. So do remember to have some music in your day; it will not only help your child, but will also help you to feel relaxed too.

The possibilities for play are endless, but it's easy to run out of ideas as a parent, so below I've suggested some good activities for the one to three age group. This is not an exhaustive list, of course – feel free to be inventive!

Creative Play

Why Creative Play is Good for Your Child

Play that involves making things, such as painting, playdough and cooking, is a great favourite with toddlers. Your child will feel very satisfied when he has created something, as it is a wonderful way to express himself. Creative play helps your child to develop fine motor skills such as holding a pencil, becoming more accurate with marks on paper, and eventually drawing recognizable objects and writing. It is good for your child to learn about textures, solids and liquids through having fun experimenting with different playthings. Playing with crayons, paints, playdough, water or sand is messy, but you need to let him have this sort of play, as he will benefit hugely from it. Creative play also relieves boredom and immediately inspires a child to get stuck into something new. If your child is tired in the afternoon, it's often worth getting out the paints or playdough to lift his spirits, and you will often have a happy child until teatime.

Remember that when your child has made something, however wonky you think it looks, it is usually very special to her, so make sure it doesn't get put in the bin by mistake. Our children used to keep their homemade things for ages and have special places to keep them. Many parents stick their child's paintings on the fridge or kitchen cupboards, and this is a nice way to display them. If your toddler is a particularly prolific artist then you could try putting a date on a few creations from each month and keeping them in a special box for her to look at when she's older.

Creative Play Ideas

Outdoors

Having a sandpit and a water-play container or paddling pool in the garden is a must if you have space. Younger toddlers will enjoy just feeling the sand and filling containers using their hands or a little spade or plastic spoon. As your child gets older he will enjoy building sandcastles using a bucket and making patterns in the sand, but he will need you to show him these new skills first. By the time your child is three, he will probably enjoy building things with sand to use in more elaborate games such as driving cars around a track or playing with dolls in a big sand fortress. It's a good idea to have a lid for your sandpit to keep it clean and dry and to put it on a sheet of plastic so you can collect all the sand that gets thrown out by excited toddlers.

Water play is always a huge hit with children. You don't need an expensive water-play table: you can use a plastic washing-up bowl or a cheap small paddling pool. Give your child a range of plastic toys or containers to play with in the water so she can experiment with pouring, splashing and making bubbles. Older toddlers will love using a plastic teapot and cups to pour imaginary drinks and may enjoy pretending to do the washing-up with plastic plates and food. Never leave your child unattended when playing with water, as children can drown in a very small amount of water.

Children also love to help with gardening and to have their own little patch of garden if you have the room. You can give your child a small trowel or plastic spade and let him help you dig and plant things. Children always seem to enjoy helping to water plants, and you can get small plastic watering cans that are just the right size. Most toddlers don't have the patience for planting seeds and waiting for things to grow until they are nearly three, as they will not be old enough to understand what it is all about. Keep a close eye on your toddler when he's 'helping' with the gardening, as he may often pull the heads off flowers or trample on plants. If you have a bird table, most toddlers will enjoy helping to put food out and watching the birds coming for a snack.

Another thing our children loved was to put little creatures from the garden in a jam jar, feed them and watch them grow. Caterpillars and worms were favourites. They need a lid on the jar with holes in it so they can breathe, and they need to be on a leaf or a plant so they have something to eat. After a few weeks, if you are lucky, a caterpillar will turn into a chrysalis and then into a butterfly or a moth. Young children love to see this happening.

Indoors

If the weather is wet or you don't have a suitable outside space, your child can still enjoy water play at the sink once she can stand up securely. Make sure the chair or step-stool cannot slip if your child is standing up at the sink. You will need to keep a close eye on her and may want to put her in a plastic apron, and it's a good idea to protect your floor with towels or a plastic sheet. Turn the taps firmly off, move any crockery and cutlery away and give your child some plastic plates, toys and containers to play with. Older toddlers love to pretend that they are doing the washing-up, so you can give her a brush and some bubbles. You can buy plastic aprons with sleeves, which are great for water play, painting and cooking.

Drawing and painting are firm favourites with young children, and they love to see that they can create something on paper all by themselves. If you're not a big fan of mess, try starting with crayons or coloured pencils. Your child will just scribble for quite a while but will be very pleased with himself, so encourage him and tell him that it's a lovely drawing. By around two, your child may be telling you what his drawing is, though it won't usually look very accurate! Older toddlers become better at drawing and may draw a recognizable person with a head and two legs. One fun idea using crayons is to do rubbings: put a small flat object such as a leaf under some paper and help your child to scribble over it with the edge of the crayon to see the pattern come through. Greaseproof paper works very well for this.

All children love to paint, and the more mess the better! In my experience, it's best to do painting when you have a good stretch of time and you're not in a hurry, as you need some time to prepare and your child will probably be so absorbed by it that she won't want to stop in a rush. If your child is painting on a table, it's a good idea to cover the surface with a plastic tablecloth or a newspaper. Put your child in old clothes or a plastic apron to protect her clothes. You can buy a range of different paints for children, but the main things to check are that they are water-soluble (and therefore easy to wash off) and non-toxic. If you put water on the table for washing brushes, use a small container such as an eggcup or yoghurt pot to avoid big spillages. Try not to worry too much if your child mixes paint colours together or adds lots of water to the paint, as this is all part of experimenting and learning. Your child can paint with a chunky brush, with sponges or with her fingers, and older toddlers like to make prints with different objects or shapes cut out of a potato or pressed into plasticine. Once your child has finished a painting, you can hang it outside or over the bath to dry if it's quite wet.

Playdough is another thing children love, as they enjoy the texture of it and like to squeeze it to see what happens to it. Younger toddlers will just enjoy prodding, poking and rolling playdough and older toddlers will be able to use cutters and start to model shapes with their hands. You can buy plastic playdough machines, which your child can feed the playdough into so that it comes out in all sorts of different shapes. Playdough is very easy to make, and the home-made version keeps well in the fridge.

Recipe for playdough

2 cups plain flour
1 cup salt
2 teaspoons cream of tartar
2 cups cold water
2 tablespoons cooking oil
A few drops of food colouring

1. Put all ingredients except the food colouring in a bowl and mix together.
2. Cook well in a heavy-bottomed saucepan until the dough peels off the side of the pan.
3. Cool on a surface and knead well, adding drops of food colouring.
4. Roll it up and keep it in the fridge in a plastic box or bag.

Children also love sticking things to make pictures, and this is quite an easy thing to do. You can buy packets of different-shaped stickers or get them free with children's magazines. When our children were young we had scrapbooks so that they could cut out pictures and stick them in, perhaps to remember special trips or days out. There are many different types of glue, so look around and find one that suits you. A solid glue that comes in a stick is best for younger toddlers, and then when your child is getting the hang of sticking you can move on to PVA glue. Be aware, though, that your child may try to stick together everything he can lay his hands on. You can buy a pair of children's scissors, which have rounded ends and are safe and easy for older toddlers to use. When cutting, he will need some help from you to start with, and it is a good idea to give him little pieces of paper to cut out before you move on to something thicker like card. Children also love to make cut-out models from old cereal boxes or bits of cardboard; this again is creative and will keep your child happy for some time.

Children nearly always love to help you cook, although you may find that young toddlers suddenly lose interest and go off to play with something else. I think it is a very important part of a child's development to be allowed to help in the kitchen. If you are having problems with your child eating, I often find that encouraging her to stand up beside you when you are mixing food and have little tastes helps her to recognize that food is good and fun. You can buy children's rolling pins, shaped biscuit cutters and little sweets to go on cakes. Making things like jam tarts is a good place to start, as she can help make the pastry and then use her rolling pin to roll a little bit out for herself. You can help her cut a few tarts out with a pastry cutter and then help her to spoon the jam in. When they are cooked make sure she doesn't eat any until they are properly cooled, as jam does get incredibly hot.

I used to make all my own bread when the children were growing up and they loved standing up at the table kneading it with me. If you don't have time to make bread from scratch you could buy a bread mix and have fun with your child kneading it and making it into different shapes. Most children enjoy decorating a cake or buns and it can be really special for them to help with a birthday cake. You can make a smoothie or a milkshake with soft fruit, yoghurt and milk (or ice cream if you're feeling naughty) and this can be a good way of encouraging your toddler to have some fruit.

Whenever you are cooking with your toddler, always keep him away from the stove and hot liquids, as accidents can happen so quickly. If you are cooking with several children you need to set it all up first and make absolutely sure of safety measures.

Indoor gardening is another fun activity. Even if you don't have a garden, you can try growing some plants from seed indoors with your toddler. We used to keep seeds from fruit when our children were little and tried to grow plants from them. Cress and fruit seeds grow very quickly in little pots, and you could try making a miniature garden in an old baking dish or tinfoil tray. Collect stones, small plants and sticks and so on, and let your child arrange them on some soil. You can then plant seeds or small plants in the soil, and you could have a 'pond' made out of a plastic lid with some water in it.

Active Play

Why Active Play is Good for Your Child

I cannot stress too much the importance of active play for your child. Active play in whatever form is the basis for an active lifestyle in the future. Childhood obesity is rising at an alarming rate, so as parents we need to take active play seriously and give our children as much opportunity as possible to run around and play outside. A healthy child has lots and lots of energy; in fact, you will probably at times wish you had some of it too. Active play is good for your child's general health and particularly for her heart and lungs, as they have to work harder when she is dashing around. Active play burns up many more calories than 'sitting-down' play activities and so helps to prevent obesity.

Physical activity relieves tension and helps prevent stroppiness in your child, as he can let off steam by running around, kicking a ball or going for a good walk. Toddlers who have had plenty of active play eat well, sleep well and are generally contented. My motto when our children were young was to take them out for a walk every day if possible, even if the weather was bad. I would dress them up in their wet-weather gear and off we would go. It made a big difference, not only to the children but to me as well, as we all got some fresh air and I was able to clear my head too. Sadly, today we live in a society where children often don't play outside very much, so try to spend time with your child playing outdoors whenever you can.

Your child will have a great sense of achievement and independence as you let her run around the park or playground, although she will usually watch to make sure you are there for her. Taking your child out to play with other children will also develop her social skills and help her to learn how to play with others. In fact, you'll notice that the main way young children play together is by just rushing around, whether in the playground or at a toddler group.

Ideas for Active Play

There will be times when your child needs to let off steam in the house, either because of the weather or if you just aren't able to go out. Surprisingly, active play can work quite well in the house, so don't be afraid to have a go. When our children were young they would zoom round and round the table after supper on ride-on toys in the winter when it was dark and they couldn't play outside. This was great, as it would wear them out before their bath and bedtime. If you have room in your house this is a good way for children to play for a little while. Children also love building camps and assault courses with cushions that they can climb over and have rough-and-tumble play in. You could also put a dry paddling pool inside and fill it with little plastic balls similar to the balls you get in indoor play areas. Most toddlers love dancing to music, and you could let them dance along to a television programme or a CD of their favourite music.

Playing in the garden or park opens up endless ideas for active play at all times of the year. As your toddler's motor skills develop, he will enjoy running, jumping, hopping and skipping on a soft surface such as grass or a rubber-crumb playground. Ball games such as football or just rolling or bouncing a ball are great fun too. If your garden is big enough you could buy a football net for your toddler to kick the ball into as he gets older and his skills become more accurate. Out in the garden or park, children often enjoy pushing toy buggies or prams, or riding tricycles or other ride-on toys. It is interesting to watch older toddlers play, as you will often notice that from around two years most little girls choose a pram and most little boys choose a tractor or digger if there is a choice. Many toddlers love to climb and crawl, so climbing frames and slides are a great favourite at the park. You could even build an assault course from large cardboard boxes in your garden.

Taking your child out to play in big open spaces such as fields and woods is good for her, as it gives her a completely new experience of openness and freedom that she wouldn't get from a walk down the street or in the park. If you live near any hills, older toddlers will love to climb up and roll down them. If you live near a beach you could go there out of season and let your child have a good run or a game of football on the sand. It is good for all children to have the chance to run in wide open spaces, and to be taken out in the wind and the rain to experience the different feelings of the elements. When it rains, try taking your toddler out to splash in puddles in some boots. If it snows, go out in the snow and build a snowman. You could even give your toddler a little shovel to help you clear the path.

Swimming is another great activity for toddlers, especially if you live near a good indoor pool. You will be amazed how tired your child gets when you take him swimming, but it is a wonderful form of exercise. Always make sure your child has armbands (water-wings) or a swimming costume with built-in floats when you go swimming. If you enjoy horse-riding, your toddler can have pony rides and even lessons by the time he is three years old. This is a lovely activity, as your child begins to learn about caring for an animal as well as having fun and taking exercise.

Pretend Play

Why Pretend Play is Good for Your Child

Pretend or imaginative play is very important for your child and is part of her normal development. Pretend play is a toddler's way of making sense of the world, and it helps her imagination to develop and gradually increases her independence in play. Your child may need a little guidance when she is a young toddler, but by the time she is three years old she will have wonderful imaginative games and even pretend people that she plays with. You may find that your child goes into a little world of her own, and if you disturb her she may look quite embarrassed that you have seen her at play. It is important that as parents we don't interfere and try to get our children to play in the way we think they should. Let your child have unstructured play whenever she wants to, and try not to make too many suggestions that dictate the 'script' of the pretend play. Toddlers need imaginative games, as they can then be 'number one' and can boss their teddies and dolls around and tell them what to do.

You will notice that your young toddler will initially copy everyday domestic activities that he has seen going on around him since he was born, such as housework or cooking. This helps him to make sense of his world and to develop his social and physical skills. All our children used to love to play at cooking and make me wonderful meals. As he gets older your child's play will become more complex and he will often make up elaborate play scenarios with other children. Dressing up in adult clothes and wearing hats is another way for your child to escape into fantasy play. You will often notice your child talking out loud to a make-believe person who is very real to him, or talking to his doll or teddy in a funny voice. All this helps to develop his social skills and enables him to play and get on with other children well.

Imaginative play helps your child to learn about expressing her emotions, for instance by cuddling her teddy or doll to make it better. This type of play also helps toddlers work through worries about the unknown, for example playing doctors or mummies and daddies when a new baby is on the way. Toddlers will normally play the part of one of the parents and a doll or teddy will be the new baby. Allow your toddler time for imaginary games that give vent to different emotions and ideas. Sometimes she will want you to join in and at other times she will want you to leave the room so that she can get on and play. Often older siblings are ideal partners in imaginative play.

Pretend Play Ideas

A toddler of a year old will have very limited concentration compared with a child of three and will often use toys as props in the early stages of pretend play. A garage and cars or a farmyard and animals to go with it will be the sorts of things he uses to have imaginary games. Young toddlers will love to 'cook' and have pretend tea parties, which can be great fun for you to join in with. You can either buy toy crockery and cooking things for your child or let him play with plastic kitchen equipment and wooden spoons from the kitchen.

As your child gets older she will want more stimulating pretend play scenarios. Playing shops is a great game and a 'shop' can be easily made from old cardboard boxes, tins and packets of food. You and your child can take turns at being the shopkeeper and customer, or have friends round to play in the shop. Your child will probably enjoy dressing up and pretending to be Mummy or Daddy, or a teacher if she is going to preschool. She could play doctors and nurses, or be a vet and make some toy animals better. It is a good idea to have a dressing-up box that you get out from time to time. You can add old clothes, scarves, gloves, bags and hats to it, and bits of old non-valuable jewellery. Jumble sales are good if you need to stock up on these things.

Building dens is one of the things that young children love to do, having their own 'secret' space. You can do this by using a couple of chairs or a clotheshorse and draping blankets over them so that your child can crawl inside and play. Toddlers love doing this, especially if there are other children playing too. Our children used to play trains and go on journeys on the stairs, with bags to put their toys in that they were taking with them. As they got bigger, if it was a wet day they would have their tea on the stairs too, or have it in their 'camp'. You could try giving your child a picnic tea in his camp with some finger food.

Making camps or dens in the garden is always great fun. Outside pretend play is open to all sorts of imagination, and you could get a playhouse for the garden or a little tent. We have a plastic shop that fits together so that children can play inside, and our grandchildren love this. You can often get wonderful second-hand toys for the garden from second-hand shops or internet sites such as Freecycle or eBay.

People sometimes ask me what I think about letting a child play with a toy gun. I have to say that when our children were growing up they did have a little toy gun and some caps to fire with it. This was fairly normal for children to have at that time. However, society has changed and today guns, shooting and killing are constantly in the pages of our newspapers and have sadly become a reality of life. If our children were growing up today we would not buy them toy guns to play with. Having said that, I don't think that will stop children from using sticks and playing with them as pretend guns, and I don't see any harm in children doing this as part of their imaginative play. Normally this sort of play is very harmless, and it is part of children wanting to have active play in which they can be a hero or a 'baddie'.

Developmental Play

All play is educational – and all is important to your child's development. Your child will learn just as much tipping some rice from one container into another as she will trying to do a puzzle. Having said that, there are some good activities and toys that will start to prepare your child for nursery and school. Setting out a little table and chair or a desk for your child is a great idea, as she can sit and do puzzles, crayoning or anything that involves fine motor skills. This is often a good idea if you have a younger sibling crawling around spoiling her game, or if your child needs some quiet time in the day just concentrating on an absorbing activity.

Stacking cups are a wonderful toy for toddlers of all ages. Most toddlers will need help to build them into a tower in the right order, but will be able to experiment with putting different sizes inside each other and building small towers. Simple shape-sorters and puzzles with pull-out pieces are also great for toddlers, improving their motor skills and their ability to match shapes, as well as helping them to problem-solve when something doesn't fit.

Having plenty of books and reading to your child is one of the best educational things that you can do. You can start showing him pictures in books from a very early age, helping him to be interested in pictures and stories and talking about the words on the page. For a young toddler, simple picture books about everyday objects are perfect. Toddlers also enjoy animal books and you can practise making the animal noises with your child, which may well be some of his first few words! Once your child is showing an interest in words as well as pictures, you can point out letters and words on signs and shops, helping him to learn perhaps the letters of his name. Older toddlers will probably be starting to show an interest in colours and shapes. You can help your child to learn about these in a fun way by looking at colours or shapes in books, and seeing if you can find toys or objects around the house that match.

Most toddlers enjoy toys that bleep or play music or sounds when buttons are pressed, and in today's world children will often start using computers at preschool or nursery. However, expensive electronic toys will not give your child any better start educationally than reading plenty of good books. A good resource for older toddlers is the CBeebies website (www.bbc.co.uk/cbeebies), which has a number of games that young children can play simply by using the space bar on a keyboard, and lots of pictures and words to songs that you can print out for your child. The website features characters from a range of BBC children's television programmes and gives parents tips on which skills each game teaches.

Top Ten Toys to Last You Through the Toddler Years

Don't feel you have to buy lots of expensive toys for your child; in fact many brilliant toys can be picked up second-hand. I've chosen ten toys for toddlers that will last you from one to three years and beyond. You'll find it interesting to see how your child's play changes over the toddler years and she uses these toys in many different ways.

- *a set of stacking cups or bricks*
- *a doll or teddy*
- *lots of books – you can join your local library for variety*
- *a push-along toy such as a brick trolley or buggy*
- *a ride-on toy*
- *a train set or cars and garage*
- *play sand, either in a sandpit or washing-up bowl*
- *a tea set or plastic cups and plates from home*
- *a dressing-up box*
- *a magnetic drawing toy and/or crayons – these are great for travelling and save your house from biros and felt pens.*

CHAPTER 8

Your Toddler's Development

You will probably have noticed that the physical growth of your child slows down in his second year of life, and this continues through the toddler years; he may not grow quickly again as he did in those first three months of life until he's a teenager. However, your child will probably have occasional growth spurts, and you will find that he grows out of clothes very quickly and then settles down again. Although this is a time of slower physical growth, you will notice a huge growth in independence. He will become a very real little person who lets you know quickly what he wants! During these toddler years, your child will learn to walk and move about easily, his skills with his hands will become more refined, he will be able to express himself with language, and you will also see him develop emotionally. These years are very rewarding, exciting and happy times, as well as being exhausting, because you seem to be always on the go. Lots of parents say to me they wish they had remembered during this time that it would pass very quickly. You soon forget it as you go on to the next stage – his first day at school!

An Overview of Ages One, Two and Three

At the age of one year your child will still seem quite a baby. She may be just walking and she may have a few words or not really be talking at all yet. She will understand a huge amount of what you are saying to her even if she is not talking much. She will probably be eating the same sort of food you have and will no longer need to have it mashed up. She will be sitting up in a high chair and can join in with family meals. She should be sleeping well at night and having one good nap in the day and maybe a catnap in the afternoon. You will find that it is easier to take her out to restaurants and places to visit as she is more adaptable now, and if she doesn't get her food and nap at exactly the right time she usually will not be too bothered.

By the time your toddler is two years old he will be very active, running around and getting into everything. He will probably manage the stairs without any problem. He will usually be putting a few words together, will have many more words in his vocabulary and will be able to copy lots of new words from you. He will also understand what you are asking him, but he will be much more independent and will want to do things his way. Most two-year-olds will still need a nap during the day and should be sleeping well at night. Going out, especially to restaurants, can become more tricky during this year as your child probably won't want to sit still. Child-friendly venues with plenty of space for running around come into their own during this year.

By the time your child is three years old she will be very skilled physically and will enjoy running, jumping, hopping and skipping. She will probably be able to ride a little bike or tricycle as her co-ordination will be well developed. She will be increasingly independent and able to undress and dress herself quite well, and should be able to use the potty or toilet without much help. She will probably be very sociable by now, even if she has been shy as a younger child. During this year, your child will enjoy the stimulation of playing with other children and can start at nursery. You will be able to reason with her at this age, and she will understand almost all of what you say to her. Her vocabulary should be good, and she will usually be putting words together in sentences. A three-year-old will not usually be too restless when you're out and about, and she will often have favourite places to visit.

Remember that all children develop at different speeds and that if your child is learning to walk he probably won't be able to concentrate on learning to talk at the same time. You usually find that children only work on developing one skill at a time, but in the end they all come, and by the time he goes to school at five you will have forgotten whether he was an early or late walker, talker and so on. However, if you have any concerns about your child's development and he seems to be lagging behind other children, talk to your health visitor or doctor about this. It's much better to reassure yourself by talking to the professionals than worrying about it on your own.

Physical Development

Growth

By the time your child is one year old she will be about three times her birth weight. It is a good idea to have her weighed now and again; if you have scales at home you can put her on these and jot down what her weight is. Between the age of one and two years her weight gain will slow down and she may only put on 1.8–2.7 kg (4–6 lb) in weight. Between two and three years she will probably put on around 1.8–2.3 kg (4–5 lb) in weight. Unless your child is very underweight because she's had feeding problems or has been very ill, you don't need to keep too much of a check on how much weight she is gaining. There is less concern from health visitors about the rate of weight gain these days than there used to be. However, if you are concerned that she is not growing well or is looking too thin, then have her checked. Some children have a growth hormone deficiency, so if you are concerned ask your doctor, who will advise you on this.

Many parents worry that their toddler is overweight. I always think it is good if your child has some 'baby fat', as once he starts walking it is surprising how quickly you find the weight will come off. Also, if your child has some fat reserves this will sustain him if he is ill and goes off his food for a while. However, there has been a huge rise in childhood obesity, and it's important to be aware of this when you think about what to give your child to eat and how much activity he does. If your toddler is not very active or looks overweight despite having lots of exercise, it's important to talk to your health visitor or doctor to get advice about his weight and diet.

Your child's height will depend very much on family genes and whether you are short, medium or tall parents. By the time she is a year old, she will usually be 18–25 cm (7–10 inches) taller than when she was born. Between the age of one and two years she may grow 10–13 cm (4–5 inches) taller. Then between two and three years she will probably grow about 5 cm (2 inches) taller. Her feet will grow quite quickly in the toddler years and it is important to have them measured regularly, about every two to three months.

By the time he is twelve months old he will probably have eight teeth, four in the top and four in the bottom, so that he has a toothy grin when he smiles. During the next eighteen months he will cut the rest of his teeth in stages; some will come through with him hardly noticing them, while others will be more painful. By the time he is about two and a half, he will probably have his full set of twenty teeth. Don't worry if he hasn't got all of these, as some children's teeth come through later than others.

As I've said before, all children grow at different rates so try not to get worried if your child is smaller or taller than others. If your child was premature, she will probably lag behind in growth for a while, but will usually have caught up in size by the time she is two years old. If your child fails to put on weight or grow taller by the time she is three, and she is eating well, then it is advisable to talk to your doctor about it.

Walking

Before your child starts to walk on his own, he will walk along holding onto the furniture and also walk around his cot holding onto the bars. He will then stand unaided for a few seconds and take maybe one or two steps on his own. This is very exciting for him; he will love it and you can encourage him to do more. Many children start walking when they are about one year old, but many don't walk until they are at least eighteen months old. Some children are quite happy just to sit and crawl, and you may find that one parent was a late walker and he is taking after them. Make sure that you give him plenty of encouragement to walk, such as taking both his hands in yours and leading him, or letting him take a few steps across a small gap to reach a toy. Help him to walk round the furniture and in his cot. Praise him for trying to do it, as this will encourage him too. If your child is showing no signs of walking (such as pulling himself up on the furniture) by the time he is two years old then you need to get medical advice.

Once your child has taken her first steps, she will soon find her feet and before long she will be toddling around. She will need your hands to help her in those early days and to give her support and encouragement. Give her lots of cuddles when she falls over (as she will) but pick her up or say 'up you get' and encourage her to carry on. Once she's on her feet, you will find she can use push-along toys. We had a baby walker for our children to push around, and it really helped them learn to walk. You will find that at the beginning she will get tired from all the exercise she is doing. I am always amazed at how quickly children progress once they start to walk. For a little while they toddle and often fall; then suddenly it seems they become much more sure-footed and next they start running.

Don't worry if your child relapses into crawling again for a while after learning to walk. Some children do this because of a fall, because they are ill, or often when a new baby has arrived in the house. Sometimes your child may do this simply because he is learning to do something else and can only concentrate on learning one new thing at a time. You will find that this stage passes and he will start walking again.

From around the age of two, your child will learn how to go up and down steps by herself without falling over. She will also get quite good at carrying a toy around with her and bending down to pick things up off the ground. Gradually her confidence will increase and she will be running. This is the time when you need to keep a close eye on her so that she doesn't get out of the garden and run into the road, or run off when you are in the park. Most toddlers will not usually go far, but I always recommend using reins when you're out in a busy environment. I prefer reins to a wrist strap as I think you have more control over your child and you can often prevent her from falling by tightening the reins. You can also loosen the reins so that she doesn't think you are holding onto her. Of course your toddler must be allowed the freedom to roam and discover what is around her, but if she is walking without reins make sure you can see her and get to her quickly if she needs you.

By the time your child is three you will find he is walking well and will probably not want to go in the buggy very often unless he is tired. I would still take a buggy out with you for walks just in case he is very tired and collapses and won't walk home. Having the buggy also gives an active toddler a little time out to relax. Some children are better walkers than others and love to go out and run around, whereas others prefer the buggy. Two of our children loved walking wherever we were but our other child disliked it, and there were always battles. She grew out of it and by the time she got into her teens she loved walking, so don't give up if you have a disgruntled toddler when out for walks.

Gross Motor Skills

During the toddler years you will notice how much your child progresses with her physical skills. She will love testing her physical limits by climbing, jumping, skipping and running, and she will probably enjoy dancing to music. You will notice that her co-ordination improves as she learns to do many new things. These skills will not all come at once, and children develop at different rates. Similarly, some children are more adventurous and active than others and so get more practice! If you go to a playgroup or toddler group with your child you will notice this variation, so don't worry if your child seems to be behind others.

From about eighteen months, your child will begin to use ride-on toys, depending on when he learns to walk. He will initially need some help until he has got the hang of it. He will push dolls in prams and buggies without any trouble, lifting them in and out and putting all sorts of things into the pram. He will probably love climbing and will be able to climb up and go down a slide. Your child will love to play with a ball, the bigger the better! He will be better able to kick it than catch it when he first starts walking. As he gets more control he will throw it too. It is quite a while before a child can catch a ball, but he will put his hands out to try to catch it. He will bounce it around the garden if you have one. All this is very good exercise for him. He will also love to go swimming with you with his armbands or float-suit on.

Most children will run, jump, hop and skip very easily by the time they are three. Your child will probably seem to have boundless energy at this age. She will be better able to catch a ball during this year and will be able to throw it overarm, and she will get great enjoyment from kicking a ball around the garden. She will be able to stand on one leg and balance well, and also jump across a gap. She should be able to ride a tricycle without any trouble. By the time your child is around three she will be washing herself in the bath and be able to get in and out on her own. You must be there with her, though, just in case she slips. She will be able to dress and undress herself with a bit of help, although she may not always want to!

Fine Motor Skills

When your child is around one year old he will be able to hold a pencil or a crayon in his hand and scribble. He will also be able to clap his hands and play 'pat-a-cake' with you. He will be able to pick up quite small items and may be able to post toys into slots or a toy postbox. He may begin to build towers with bricks but probably won't have much skill with this. He will also try to put pieces of Duplo together. He will hold a spoon and may feed himself, even if some of the food ends up in his ear! He will want to hold his drinking cup and will try to do it himself. He will be very quick to throw things on the floor at mealtimes and wait for your response.

Between the ages of one and two, you will see her fine motor skills developing quite fast. She will want to do puzzles with you, and may spend some time trying to fix the pieces in the right places. She will like crayoning, 'writing' and using paints. It is a good idea to have a painting apron to protect her clothes if she gets over-enthusiastic with the paints! She will be feeding herself more and drinking from her cup well, even without a lid. You will still need to guide her in this, though. She will play well with toys that need more skill, such as a little train set or cars on a track. She will be able to wash her hands with your help and will love playing water games in the bath. You may find she stands up in her cot and takes her nappy off.

By the time your child is approaching three his motor skills will be more refined. He will be able to thread beads onto string to make a little necklace or bracelet. He will play well with Lego or Duplo and enjoy more complicated puzzles. He will hold a pen or crayon with more skill and be better able to draw within the lines of a picture. He will love to paint and make things from odds and ends. He will enjoy glueing things and will be better able to do this without getting in a mess. He should be able to feed himself well and drink from a cup or mug without a lid.

Lots of parents wonder whether their child will be left- or right-handed. If you as parents are both left-handed there is a fair chance your child will be also, but if only one of you is then the chance drops dramatically. If neither of you are left-handed then it is unlikely that she will be. All children are ambidextrous (using either hand with no preference) in the early years and handedness does not usually appear until the child is at least three years of age.

Speech Development

During the toddler years you will see your child's speech develop dramatically, from a few baby sounds and words at one year old to sentences and conversation by the time he is three years old. Younger toddlers understand far more than they can say, but by the time your child is three your child will be able to understand and join in with most adult conversation. Learning to talk is a vital part of growing up as it enables your child to communicate with those around him, and allows him to make more independent choices and decisions.

When Will My Child Start to Talk?

There is a great deal of variation in when children start to talk and parents often worry about when their child will say her first proper word. First children often start to talk earlier than their siblings as they have undivided attention from their parents, whereas a younger child may not speak so soon as they can't get a word in edgeways! Girls often start to speak earlier than boys, although most boys catch up quite quickly. Children brought up in bilingual households may also be later in speaking as they are hearing two different languages in the home, so they have more words to understand before they start to speak.

Most children will have a few recognizable words by the time they are eighteen months old, and many will have around a hundred words by the time they're two. All young children will use gestures to communicate, such as pointing or lifting up their arms to be picked up, even if they know the word. From around two they will be putting two words together in simple 'sentences' such as 'Daddy work' for 'Daddy's gone to work'. Most children will be quite competent in talking by the time they're three, but they will still make some mistakes and will have immature pronunciation. It takes many years of learning to perfect speech.

What Can I Do to Help My Child to Talk?

It is important to chat and sing to your child whenever you can, even if you feel silly doing it. You will probably have been doing this ever since he was a tiny baby. Your baby will have been cooing and blowing bubbles for some months and then making baby sounds, gradually saying 'dada' and 'mama' and maybe other sounds too. This is all part of the process of learning to talk. You may find he makes these noises for some months to come, but usually these progress into words that you can begin to understand. I cannot overestimate the importance of chatting all the time to your child; it really is the means to helping him learn to talk. Talk to your child on and off all day while you are doing things, telling him what you are doing, pointing out things of interest and repeating the names of them. Children learn speech by imitation, which is why this sort of repetition is so vital. You don't need to carry on talking in 'baby language' to your child, as he needs to hear more words and simple sentences spoken as adults would so that he can learn these words in context. It helps your child if you speak clearly and repeat the word that you are wanting him to learn, or put emphasis on it in the sentence. I don't see a problem in using such words as 'doggy' or 'moo-cow', but speak in sentences too.

From an early age you can sing nursery rhymes to her, with a CD on if that helps you. The rhythm and melody of music make it easier for your child to pick up words, and the repetition of the songs helps her to learn them. It is useful to have eye contact with your child while you sing, as this helps her to watch how you pronounce the words and to copy you. Reading books also helps your child with talking. You can buy board books when she is young, containing pictures of animals, foods and everyday objects. Say the names of the things in books and encourage your child to copy you by saying the word. As she gets older, reading a bedtime story will also help her vocabulary grow and will teach her an interest in words. You want to make reading fun, so buy books with brightly coloured pictures that she will be interested in. A child of a year will not sit still for long, so read to her for only a short time, but as she gets older she will probably enjoy talking to you about books for much longer.

Once your child starts talking, give him lots of encouragement and praise. If he makes a mistake with a word it's important not to criticize, just repeat it to him again in the right way. It takes quite a while for a child to get all of his words right, and anyway it sounds rather sweet when he says it in a funny way to start with. When he starts to say more words you can encourage him to put them together by building on his sentences. If he says 'Daddy work', say to him, 'Yes, Daddy's gone to work. He went in the car, didn't he?' It is important to give your child time to express himself. Sometimes you will find that older toddlers start to stammer as they try to get their words out. This often happens because the speech centre in his brain is working faster than he can actually say things. It's important not to make a big issue out of this or to tell your child to speak 'properly' or get cross with him, as this can make it worse. Many children go through this stage of having difficulty in getting their words out; they just need to be given time to speak and it will settle down.

What Will My Child Understand?

Your child's understanding develops first, before she begins to talk. In fact, she can understand a lot more than she can say, and you will notice this in her first year. At first she will understand single words, for example pointing to her nose, mouth or ears when you say the word or pointing to animals in a book. She will respond to actions in nursery rhymes, again following your lead at first. Then she will learn to understand simple instructions, such as 'Give it to Mummy', especially if you point or hold out your hand when you give these instructions. As her speech begins to develop, she will understand simple sentences and be able to respond to choices such as 'Do you want juice or milk?' As she gets older, she will understand more detailed instructions such as 'Can you put the sock in the washing basket for Daddy?' From about eighteen months she will begin to develop understanding of 'position' words such as 'in', 'on', 'under' and 'next to'. You will know that she can understand these when she's looking for something and you say 'It's under the table', and she duly gets down on the floor and looks under the table. Older toddlers will often pretend not to understand what you are saying when they don't like what you're asking them to do, and you will then find yourself repeating things! If you are concerned that your child does not seem to be understanding you, it is worth having her hearing checked, as it's very common for children to have mild hearing problems due to 'glue ear' or other infections.

What If My Child Isn't Talking at Two?

If your child has been exposed to speech (that is, if you as parents are not exclusively using sign language and/or your child is not deaf) and he is not making any advances in talking by the age of two, then it would be sensible to take him to your doctor for a check. One of the main causes of late-developing speech is hearing difficulties, although this should have been picked up in earlier hearing tests. Glue ear is a common problem, often causing children's speech to be delayed, and once this is treated children catch up quite quickly. If your doctor is concerned then he will refer you to a speech and language therapist for assessment and advice. Even if your child's speech is delayed, keep on talking to him and encourage him to communicate with you in any way he can. It can encourage him to use words (even if they don't sound right) if you give him simple choices such as 'Would you like the *car* or the *ball*?', emphasizing the words for him to say. There is lots of helpful advice on the website of I CAN, a charity for children with speech and language difficulties, about ways to help your child to communicate, including a free DVD for parents called 'Chatter Matters', which gives you clear tips about helping your child's speech (www.ican.org.uk).

Emotional Development

As your child enters the toddler years you will notice swings in her moods, from being happy and bubbly to being cross and very unhappy. This is perfectly normal and part of growing up. She is learning so much that at times she can hardly cope with all that is going on. Because she is now walking and very active she will get very tired and so will react in negative ways when things happen that she is not sure about. Your child will mostly be happy as long as things are going her way, but if you want her to do something she doesn't want to then she will let you know in no uncertain terms! During the toddler years, your child will become more aware of simple emotions such as happiness and sadness and will develop some empathy for how you or other children are feeling.

Happiness and Fun

One of the wonderful things about the toddler years, especially when you look back, is the sense of joy and excitement that small children feel about the simplest of things. It's worth remembering this when you're having a tough day with lots of tantrums and tiredness. Toddlers often wake up ready to greet the day with a smile and with a sense of expectancy about all the fun and playing they are going to do. These are special joyful moments for you as a family, and times that you'll look back on fondly when you're trying to extricate a grumpy teenager from his bed. Your child will probably take delight in all the new things you do with him, from painting to going on outings and simple things like playing ball together. In essence, the toddler years are all about exploration, and for the most part your child will find this great fun.

Attachment

Your toddler will have a growing awareness of the special relationship she has with you as parents. She will probably love to hug and cuddle you, and will want you when she's upset or has hurt herself. She will love to spend time with you, watching what you do and helping you. One of the best ways to show love for your child is just to be with her and involve her in what you're doing – it makes her feel special. During these years your child will also develop special bonds with her wider family, such as uncles, aunts and grandparents. If you live far away from your family, it's good to have photos of your family to talk about with your toddler and to let her talk to relatives on the phone whenever you have the chance.

Young toddlers can often be very clingy and not want you to leave them with anyone else. You may find this especially with your first child, as he is used to you doing most things with him. It is a good idea to let him go to a grandparent or a friend sometimes to begin the separation from you and your partner. If you are at home with your child and your partner is out at work all day, then let them spend time together for a while in the evenings or at weekends so that your child gets used to being without you. Clinginess seems to happen more in the second year of life, as usually by the third year he is understanding more about being with other people, making friends and looking forward to going to spend the day with someone else. Taking him to playgroups and toddler groups will help him learn to share you with others as you both mix with the families there.

Friendships

It is very important for your child to play with other toddlers, and you will notice a big change in the way she relates to other children between the ages of one and three. At first, toddlers will play side by side, seeming to hardly notice other children their age. However, if you look a little closer, you may notice your child copying what another child is doing, and this is the beginning of learning to play and be friends together. If your child seems to prefer her own company, don't worry. Let her be, as you will find that this won't last for long. Toddler groups are good at this stage to help your child to get used to the noise of other children, to play with others and to learn to share the toys. Most younger toddlers will love to play with older children and are quite fascinated by them.

By the time your child is about two, he will probably be joining in play with other children, especially ones he knows well, although you may find that they fight over toys quite a lot! This is all about learning to share and is just one of the stages that all children seem to go through. Remember that toddlers will hit out at each other very quickly if they get cross and then the tears and screams come, so you will need to be there to sort things out. As you take him to visit friends and get to know people he will make good friendships that will probably last for some years, especially if you continue to live in the same area. Around this age you may find that your child has special friends that he talks about often.

By the time your child is three, she should be mixing well with other children. She will have quite definite ideas about who her friends are and who she wants to play with. She will probably be quite independent when playing with friends, and may well be happy to be left to play at a friend's house without you there. At three, your child will probably be starting nursery and making a whole new range of friends. You may suddenly find yourself in a social whirl of children's parties and outings!

Dealing with Frustration

Toddlers find life very frustrating at times, as they are trying to do so many things independently and are also having to learn to live by adults' rules and boundaries. There will be lots of tears in the toddler years as he deals with the frustration of not being able to do some things and not being able to express himself. Frustration will often mean that your child will have a huge tantrum or be very upset and burst into tears for no apparent reason. Dealing with tantrums in young children can be exhausting, but I'm afraid it is all part of growing up. However, it will pass! (See Chapter 3 for more detail on managing tantrums.) One of the good things about this stage is that, once the source of frustration is sorted out, your child will usually be happy and playing again in no time.

The most challenging time tends to be between one and two years of age, when your child is not able to express what it is that's frustrating or upsetting her. She may seem to have a 'short fuse' and be unable to cope with things not going her way. She will need lots of loving guidance and cuddles to help her through these times, which is not always easy when you are busy and tired and it seems as though she has been miserable all day. However, by the time your child is three you will probably find that she has settled down a lot, and you can talk to her and reason with her when she is frustrated.

Fears

One of the things I've noticed in working with children is that an awareness of things being frightening seems to develop in the toddler years. You will probably notice your child reacting in a fearful way to all sorts of different situations, especially new things that he's not familiar with. Raised voices and arguments will have a big effect on your toddler, and he may cry or run away when he hears adults shouting. It is quite common for a toddler to start having nightmares or to develop fears such as being scared of the dark, or of going upstairs on his own. These fears are very real to toddlers, as their imaginations are developing so rapidly. It is important not to get cross or tell your child off if he is going through a stage of being frightened. It may seem trivial to us, but it is very real to him and he needs lots of comfort and cuddles and to know that he's safe because you are there.

Closing Thoughts

The toddler years see a huge development in skills and independence for your child, and it's a very exciting time for a parent. By the time your child is three, she will be a real person, responding to you well and making lots of her own decisions. Ideally, you will both be ready to face the next challenge of growing independence: heading off to nursery and then to school.

CHAPTER 9

General Care

During the first year of your baby's life you will have cared for his every need without really thinking twice about it. As you enter his toddler years you will continue to do the same, except during this time you will be gradually teaching him to become more independent. Helping him to clean his own teeth, brush his hair and wash himself and teaching him how to undress and dress himself is all part of this growing-up process. It's important to teach your child about keeping clean but also to get the balance right so that he isn't afraid of getting dirty. Realistically, dirt and mess are going to be part of living with an active, exploring toddler!

Cleanliness and Hygiene

Hand-washing

I think that teaching your child to wash her hands before a meal is one of the first things to do. It is a good idea to buy a step that you can put in front of the washbasin so that she can stand and reach the water and you can wash her hands. You will need to help her for some time with this. You will find that hand-washing soon becomes part of her mealtime routine, and she may even tell you off if you forget. Toddlers get very dirty when playing, especially in the garden, so be prepared for lots of dirty hands (and faces and clothes). When you start toilet training you need to wash her hands after using the potty too. Again, you are teaching her life skills here that you hope will become part of her normal routine.

- *Fill the basin with warm water.*
- *Put your child's hands in the basin.*
- *Help him to rub soap into his hands (liquid soap is good).*
- *Rinse off the soap.*
- *Help your child to dry his hands on a towel.*
- *Toddlers love running water, so don't leave him unattended, as you may come back to find a flood.*

Nappy-changing and Using the Potty

As your toddler becomes more mobile you will discover that all of a sudden she doesn't like to have her nappy changed, and she will wriggle about and try her very best to get away from you. This can soon become a game on her part, but it's often very frustrating for you and changing time can feel like a huge battle. Even though nappy-changing is more difficult, you need to clean all her creases to prevent nappy rash, so make sure you have plenty of wipes. I've come across many parents who struggle with nappy-changing with their toddler, so here are my tips for distracting or immobilizing your child while you change her nappy. Diversion and speed are of the essence!

- *If he's too big for the changing table, put him on the floor or a mat.*
- *The secret is to be as quick as possible.*
- *Have everything you need to hand.*
- *Give your child something to play with, such as a hairbrush or tube of toothpaste.*
- *Hold your child by his ankles, and lift his hips if you can to stop him rolling.*
- *Whip the nappy off and clean him with baby wipes.*
- *Put the clean nappy on as swiftly as you can.*
- *As soon as he's changed, let him stand up to get dressed.*

Once your child is using a potty, don't let her play with the contents of her potty or put her hands down the toilet. You will still need to wipe your child's bottom, as even if she helps she will not be able to do it properly yet. Help her to wash her hands so that this becomes normal when using the toilet. Keep your child's potty clean by rinsing it out with warm water and cleaning with a toilet brush and bleach or toilet cleaner. Store the potty in the bathroom so that it's not a plaything. If you need to use a potty downstairs, it's best to put it somewhere where you can clean the floor easily, such as the downstairs toilet (see Chapter 6 for more detail).

Bathtime

I think bathtime is great fun with young children, and it is a great time for you as parents to spend some one-to-one time with your toddler. Children usually love having a bath and will enjoy experimenting with water toys all through their childhood years. Toys that stick onto the side of the bath are fun as well. Some families bath together, with parents going in the bath with the children. You don't need to bath your child every day, but I personally think it is a good idea if you can do this as part of the bedtime routine.

There are a few points to consider about your toddler's safety in the bath, as young children move very quickly and can fall easily and drown in very little water. You still also need to be careful about the temperature of the water and the taps themselves. Here are my tips for a safe, fun bathtime:

- *Be prepared to get quite wet! A plastic apron can come in handy.*
- *Never leave your child unattended in the bath.*
- *Be extra careful if you're bathing children together.*
- *A non-slip rubber mat is a must.*
- *If you don't have a mixer tap, run cold water first, then add hot water.*
- *Test the water temperature before your child gets in.*
- *Make sure the bath is warm enough, as he can get cold quickly,.*
- *Cover the hot tap with a flannel if it's hot to the touch.*
- *Make sure the taps are off tightly so your child can't scald himself.*

Some children love to have a shower, and they can go in together if you have several children. Again, don't leave your child unattended. You may find a shower is easier than a bath, especially if you can move the shower head to a low position so that your child can sit down. You can then help her to wash herself with the shower. If the controls for your shower are within reach of your toddler, take extra care that she does not turn very hot water onto herself.

Some young children may become very fearful in the bath or shower, often for no apparent reason. Sometimes it is the noise of the water running or draining away. Sometimes they may have slipped and become frightened. If your child goes through a stage of not wanting to go in the bath or shower and is obviously frightened, then just put a small amount of water in the bath with his toys. If that doesn't work, take him into the bath with you and hold him to you and play games. Usually this fear of water doesn't last for very long; be patient and it will pass.

Washing and Skin Care

During the second year of life your child will probably be interested in washing herself, so let her do this and help her when you can. It is sweet to see your child in the bath with her flannel or sponge washing herself. What you put in your child's bath will depend on her skin type and your personal preference. I know bubble baths are fun, but if your child has eczema or a sensitive skin then these products are not a good idea. Aqueous cream is a good bath product and you can wash your child with this too. You can buy soaps for eczema, or use ordinary soap if your child's skin is not sensitive. If you use oil in the bath be careful, as it will make the bath very slippery and she can easily fall over. Wash your child's body, paying particular attention to her bottom if she is still in nappies. As a general rule, don't wash your child's face with soap unless she has painted it with something or has food stains on it. Wash her face carefully with a flannel, especially if she has sensitive skin. When toddlers are teething they often get sore skin from a runny nose or dribbling, so take extra care if this happens.

After a bath or shower, you may like to use a good moisturizing cream on his body and a cream for his face, especially if he has a sore mouth or nose. Use a good barrier cream for his bottom. If he is sore or has nappy rash, don't let it go unattended. Toddlers often get nappy rash when teething, and if left this can be very painful. Children can get also get thrush on their bottoms, which will need treatment from a doctor. I still love the smell of Johnson's baby powder, but I know that many parents don't like to use powder today. The most important thing is to keep your child's skin clean and healthy.

Hair-washing

Most toddlers will go through a stage of not wanting their hair washed. Some children love it but many others do not like having water over their faces, and can become quite frightened when you mention hair-washing. I had this experience with all my three children, and found one of the best ways to help was to tell them stories of what I was finding in their hair as I washed it. I would tell them stories about little animals, probably because we were farming and that was closest to their hearts! Although we still had some battles, the distraction of the story often worked. If your child doesn't like hair-washing, try to stay relaxed, as this will pass.

To wash your toddler's hair with minimum fuss:

- *Lay your child down with your arm under her shoulder for support.*
- *Tip her head back and wet her hair with bathwater.*
- *Put on some shampoo and lather.*
- *Let her have a folded flannel over her eyes.*
- *Rinse her hair thoroughly with clean water from a jug or the shower.*
- *Older toddlers can sit up and look up at the ceiling while you rinse.*
- *Dry hair with a towel – most toddlers are scared of hairdryers!*

There are many good baby hair products on the market, and it is up to you and your personal taste as to what you use. You don't need to wash your child's hair every day unless he is going through the stage of putting food everywhere; once or twice a week is perfectly acceptable. If a little girl is frightened of having her hair washed, it is a good idea to keep her with a short hairstyle as it is then easier to wash. If she has tangly or curly hair then use a conditioner, as this will help when combing her hair. You will need a good hairbrush that is firmer than a baby brush, and you may also need a comb. Wash these when you wash your child's hair.

Cradle cap is another thing that seems to creep up quickly if left unattended. This can be caused by leftover shampoo if you haven't rinsed thoroughly. If cradle cap builds up, don't be tempted to pick it off as this can cause infection. The best way to clear it up is to use baby oil or olive oil on cotton wool and rub it into the scalp, leave it on for a few hours or overnight and then wash it off, or comb it off if the cradle cap is very thick. You will find that by doing this the cradle cap gradually comes off. Prevention is better than cure, so keep an eye on it and use some oil if you see cradle cap starting.

Fiddly Bits: Ears, Fingers and Toes

Now that your child is a toddler you can use cotton buds to clean his ears with care. Put him on your lap, give him something to play with to take his mind off what you are doing and then carefully clean his ears. This doesn't need to be done every day, maybe once a week. Cutting finger- and toenails can be rather a battle, as usually young children don't like having this done. Again, put him on your lap facing away from you, as you can hold his hand easily this way. Do his toes while he is sitting this way as well. It's good to distract him in some way, and I often find that telling stories is a great way of taking children's minds off what is happening. Use baby nail-scissors if you can, and don't cut too near the skin, as children seem to bleed easily. Cut fingernails in a rounded way in the shape of his fingertips; toenails should be cut straight across. If he wriggles a lot or gets upset, you could try using an emery board until he will sit still for you.

Dental Care

Many parents ask me when they should start cleaning their child's teeth.

I think it is a good idea to buy a little toothbrush and special children's toothpaste as soon as your child has a few teeth to help her form good brushing habits. Start by cleaning her teeth after a bath at night and then after breakfast, and this will soon become part of her daily routine. You will need to brush your child's teeth for her to start with, and then help her to do it as she gets older. Hold your child's hand, guiding the brush gently backwards and forwards and up and down. Keep the toothbrush in a mug or holder with the toothpaste so it doesn't get taken round the house and dropped on the floor or used as a toy. Change her toothbrush after about three months, or sooner if it looks battered.

Another question parents ask me is when they should first take their child to a dentist. This is really up to you, but most dentists will probably not do a full check-up on a child until he is around three and has his full set of twenty teeth. Look for a dentist who is good with young children and who will guide you into looking after your child's teeth. It is a good idea to take your child along to the dentist with you so that he can get used to it before his first check-up. Let him sit on your lap and make it a fun visit.

To help your child to have healthy teeth:

- *Clean her teeth twice a day from an early age.*
- *Avoid lots of sugary snacks and sweets.*
- *Avoid fizzy drinks.*
- *Avoid too many sweet drinks.*
- *Move from a bottle to a cup as soon as possible.*
- *Don't let your child carry a cup around to sip all day.*
- *Include plenty of calcium-rich foods in her diet.*
- *If your child has discoloured or crooked teeth, take her to the dentist.*

Clothing and Shoes

What Should My Child Wear?

Your child's clothing is your personal choice, but it's a good idea to have clothes that are easy to get on and off, especially when you are potty-training. It is probably best to avoid zips and small buttons if you are wanting to get trousers on and off quickly. When your child is learning to dress himself it is better if his clothes are easy to put on and take off without a battle. Elastic waistbands are a good idea, as are poppers and wide neck holes. Vests with poppers underneath are practical for young toddlers, as they help hold nappies in place. Once you're potty-training you might want to change to a separate vest and pants. Most toddlers are very active, so you'll need hard-wearing, practical clothes that will last well in the wash.

Layers of clothing are a good idea for young children, as you can strip off or add layers depending on the temperature. In cold weather your child will need more clothing to be snug and warm when you take her out. Remember that young children lose heat quickly and need gloves and hats when the weather is cold. Many children don't like wearing hats or gloves and you will find that no sooner have you put them on than your child has taken them off again, and searching for gloves becomes a regular pastime. I always had our children's gloves on a cord threaded through the arms of their coat so that they couldn't lose them. Personally, I would only insist on a child wearing a hat and gloves if the weather is very cold. You can buy lovely furry boots for children, and of course they need little wellington boots for wet weather. A good jacket for the rain is essential if you are taking your child out walking and she is not in the buggy all the time. In hot weather, lightweight cotton clothes will keep your child cool and also protect her from the sun. If your child is wearing short sleeves or only a vest, make sure she has plenty of sunblock on. Your child will need a sunhat, and you can buy hats in UV-protective fabric that cover the head and neck, which are great for the beach or garden. Again, layers of clothing are good for the summer so that if there's a breeze or the sun goes in you can put a cardigan or jacket on her.

From about eighteen months you may find that your child doesn't fit into sleepsuits for nightwear. There are some lovely pyjamas and nightdresses available, and your child will probably feel quite grown-up buying his first proper pyjamas! It's nice to have a dressing gown and slippers for breakfast or after bathtime. If you haven't invested in one yet, you may find a baby sleeping bag useful, as your toddler will probably wriggle at night and kick his covers off. If you do use a sleeping bag, make sure you don't overheat your child; he may only need a vest in the summertime.

Should My Child Choose Her Own Clothes?

It's good to teach your child to make some choices about her clothing, but you'll want to avoid a daily battle over what she wears. I knew a little boy who only wanted to wear his Spiderman outfit all the time, even when going out. It's quite normal for toddlers to decide they want to wear a swimsuit in the middle of winter or boots in the height of summer, or simply put horrible combinations together! When my children were growing up, my way around this was to lay out their clothes the night before, and this seemed to work quite well. If you want to give your child some choice, you could involve her by getting out a couple of tee-shirts and letting her choose which one she'd like for the next day. Your child will need guidance as to what she wears for quite some time, and doing this will make it easier when the time comes for her to wear a school uniform.

Learning to Dress and Undress

Once your child is walking, it's a good idea to encourage him to help out when you dress and undress him. He can help to pull his socks off, or lift his arms up to take a tee-shirt off. As he gets older, you will find that he'll want to do more of this independently. Leave plenty of time when getting dressed so that he can try to do it himself, as the more you try to hurry him, the more stressed you both become. Some children are more interested in dressing themselves than others, and if you find your child wants you to do it all, try to encourage him by making a game of it. Once your child has learned to undress himself, don't be surprised if he wants to strip off and run around naked at inappropriate times, as this is all part of the fun for him.

Keeping Clothes Clean

Your toddler's clothes will get messy, especially if she is out in the garden playing or feeding herself, and you will find she needs clean clothes regularly. Bibs or plastic aprons come in very handy for protecting your child's clothes. If your child hasn't got dirty then it's perfectly all right to wear the same outfit for a couple of days. Most children's clothes are easy to care for and can go in the washing machine without the need for ironing; just check the washing and drying instructions. I personally use non-biological detergent and fabric softener for children's clothes, as these are less likely to cause skin allergies.

Shoes

Your child doesn't really need shoes until he is walking. Bare feet are the best for learning to walk, but if the weather is cold you can buy slipper-socks with a gripper sole or soft crawling shoes to stop him slipping. Shopping for shoes can be a nightmare, as for some reason many children dislike trying on shoes, and once you get them in the shoe shop they can throw a real tantrum! In spite of this it is important that you have your child's feet measured properly, as his feet are growing and you don't want to hinder this in any way. His socks and shoes need to fit well and not be too tight, and there should always be a little space at the end of the shoe beyond your child's toes.

Your child only needs one pair of shoes to start with, as you'll find her feet grow very quickly and it can be an expensive business to buy more than one pair. It's probably not advisable to buy second-hand shoes as every child's feet grow in a different shape. Feet should be measured every two to three months, but you need to keep an eye on her shoes and check that her toes are not squashed in. Shoes that fasten with Velcro are good for children as they are easy to get on and off.

Haircuts

Your child will probably not need a haircut before the age of one, and when he does he may only need a tidy-up, which you may well find you can easily do yourself. If you do cut your child's hair be careful, as toddlers are very quick, and you don't want any accidents. If your child's hair needs a properly styled cut then take him to the hairdresser. Usually the hairdresser will have a special child's seat so that he can sit and look at himself in the mirror, or you may find it easier to hold him on your lap; this should keep him still for a few minutes. Haircuts are not something you need to feel you must rush to get done, so try to pick the right moment, not when he is grumpy and needing a sleep. I think the first haircut is always very exciting and rather special, and I kept a lock of hair from all of my children.

Exercise

Obesity is increasingly becoming a problem among young children, so it is important that children have plenty of exercise. Most toddlers have masses of energy and need to use this up somehow. Children who go out and play actively during the day are more ready for bed at bedtime, and sleep better too. One of the best things to do is to take your child out for a good walk, on a daily basis if you can. As soon as she is steady on her feet, she can get out of the buggy once you're in a safe place; it is so good for children to be able to explore in their own little world. When my children were growing up I took them out every day if I could. We were fortunate to be farming so we lived in the country and the walks were good. We had plenty of places to go and things to do. I am a great believer in taking children out whatever the weather (almost) and I used to dress mine up in wet-weather gear, and we would go out and find puddles to splash in. As they got older they would make camps and treehouses, and we would have picnics in the summer. Wherever you live, children benefit from walks and outdoor play.

Most children look forward to going out to play in a park or playground. Children love running around, going from swing to slide to climbing frame to see-saw. Your toddler can run, jump, hop, skip and climb when you take her out. This is all good exercise for developing her motor skills. There are probably child-friendly parks in your neighbourhood where you can go and meet your friends. I'm aware that today things are not as safe as they were when my children were growing up, and there is not the freedom today to let your children play by themselves, so keep them near you and make sure they are in sight at all times.

If they fit in with your daily life, toddler groups or sports activities for children are great fun for both you and your child. Don't feel you have to have something booked for every day, though, as this can tire everyone out! Swimming is a firm favourite and a great activity for toddlers in all weathers. Armbands or a float-suit are a good investment to help your child feel confident in the water. When the weather's not too good, indoor activities come into their own and can be a good social time for you and your child. If you can't get out, try putting on some music or a dance DVD so your child can jump and dance around, or make a cushion assault course.

Safety at Home

However childproof your house and garden are, remember that toddlers are great explorers and will often find their way into all sorts of mischief. It's good to let your child explore, and I sometimes feel we've gone overboard worrying about the safety of our children. However, toddlers really have no sense of danger until they are older, so you will need to protect them from situations in which they could be harmed. Don't leave your child unattended for a long stretch, and never leave a toddler alone with a young baby.

The majority of children's injuries happen in the home, so it's a good idea to be aware of the dangers in your home and take preventative measures. However, as with all things, there's a balance to be struck, and I'm not going to suggest you wrap your coffee table in cotton wool so that your child doesn't bang her head on it. Below are some areas to consider when looking at your home to prevent common accidents.

Safety in Play

Fall Hazards

- *Use stairgates, particularly at the top of the stairs.*
- *Watch your child carefully when he goes up and down stairs.*
- *Teach your child to hold on to the banister going upstairs.*
- *Teach your child to come downstairs on his bottom or crawling backwards.*
- *Make sure your child can't climb up to open windows, especially in his bedroom.*
- *Use window locks where necessary.*
- *If you have a balcony, don't let your child play there unattended.*
- *Keep a close eye on your child when he is climbing on furniture.*
- *Strap your child into his high chair or booster seat.*
- *Clean up any spillages on hard floors to avoid your child slipping.*
- *Make sure your child can't climb out of his cot and hurt himself.*
- *Keep the landing light on if your child is able to get out of bed.*

Bumps and Bruises

All toddlers will get bumps and bruises from time to time. However, you can prevent really painful knocks by thinking about the following:

- *If you have glass doors, put stickers on them at eye level so your child doesn't walk into them.*
- *If you have a glass-topped table, protect the corners with plastic covers.*
- *Don't let your child play with doors, to avoid getting her fingers trapped.*
- *If you have a toybox with a lid, make sure your child cannot close the lid on her fingers or climb in and get stuck.*
- *Make sure your child can't pull heavy items onto herself.*
- *Put child safety locks on any cupboards you don't want her to open.*

Choking Hazards

- *Don't leave your toddler unattended while eating.*
- *Don't let your child put large pieces of food in his mouth.*
- *Be particularly careful with foods such as lollipops or hard sweets.*
- *Encourage your child to sit down while eating.*
- *Keep small toys out of the reach of young children.*
- *Don't let your child play with crayons or pens unattended.*

Poisonous/Dangerous Substances

- *Keep household cleaners and chemicals out of reach, or in a cupboard with a child safety lock.*
- *Keep alcohol out of the reach of children.*
- *Keep medicines in a locked cupboard.*
- *Don't let your child play in the toilet or with the toilet brush.*
- *If you smoke, don't leave ashtrays or cigarettes within reach of your child. Ideally, do not smoke around your child at all.*

Burns or Scalds

- *If you have an open fire or a gas or electric fire, always use a fireguard.*
- *Never leave a hot drink within reach of your toddler.*
- *Make sure your child cannot turn hot water taps on.*
- *Always fill the bath with cold water first if you don't have a mixer tap.*
- *Teach your child not to touch the iron, oven or radiators (if very hot).*

Fiddling with Things

- *Keep electrical equipment such as televisions, videos and DVD players out of reach, or teach your child that he is not allowed to touch them.*
- *Use plastic socket covers for electrical sockets.*
- *Make sure you can unlock your doors from both sides.*
- *Tuck away electrical cords for table lamps, phones and so on.*
- *Keep possible hazards such as sewing baskets away from your child.*
- *Don't let your child play with the cords on window blinds.*
- *Make sure your child cannot reach small or dangerous items from his cot.*
- *Avoid putting hazardous objects such as plastic bags in the wastepaper basket where your child can easily find them.*

Safety and Hygiene in the Kitchen

Of all the places in the home, the kitchen probably has more hazards for young children than anywhere else. You're often busy when you're in the kitchen, so it's worth thinking about potential dangers beforehand and keeping a watchful eye on your child when you're in the kitchen together.

When you are cooking, it's a good idea to use the burners at the back of the hob so that hot pans are not within reach of your child. Make sure that pan handles are turned inwards over the stove. If you're using the oven, keep your child at a safe distance when opening the door and teach her not to touch the oven or hob. If your child is helping you to cook, take particular care that she cannot touch anything hot. Microwaved food can be very hot so make sure you keep it out of reach and stir it well before you serve it to your child to avoid any 'hot spots'. Do not have your child's high chair near hot kitchen equipment as she can easily get burned. Keep electric kettles well out of reach, and make sure that the flex from the kettle does not hang over the worktop.

You will probably want to put child safety locks on most of your kitchen cupboards, perhaps keeping one unlocked with plastic or wooden equipment that he can open and play with. Keep your washing powder, dishwasher tablets and kitchen cleaners in a high cupboard, as some children eventually work out how to open child locks. Take particular care to keep sharp knives, scissors and tin openers safely out of your child's reach. When you're in the kitchen, keep a close eye on your child to make sure he doesn't try to get into the washing machine or tumble dryer – for some reason the little doors seem to appeal to small children!

Children seem to love bins, so keep your kitchen bin out of reach if possible or teach your child that she's not allowed to touch it. If you have pets, don't let your child play with their food or drink bowls. Keep your kitchen floor clean, as your child will play here a lot, and traces of food and general dirt can harbour germs. It is important to keep the worktops in your kitchen clean, using an antibacterial cleaner. One of the main places to harbour germs is your child's high chair, so try to wipe it down straight after each meal (when it is easier to clean than after a few hours when the food is stuck on) and wipe it thoroughly with an antibacterial cleaner once a day.

Safety Outdoors

Garden Safety

Toddlers love to play outside in the garden. However, you will need to keep a watchful eye on your child, especially when he's confidently walking around and exploring. Your garden needs to be fenced, with a secure gate so that your child cannot get out onto the road. If you have a pond, this should be fenced and/or have a safety cover. If you have a paddling pool, don't leave your child unattended in the water. Sandpits need to be covered over when not in use so that pets don't use them as a toilet. Similarly, make sure your lawn is free from dog or cat droppings before your child plays in the garden. Make sure your child can't climb up onto any garden furniture and then fall off it. Your toddler will be very interested in plants and flowers as he gets older, and you will have to teach him not to pull them up and eat them. He will also probably find insects and stones to fiddle with, and you'll have to make sure these don't go in his mouth. Keep garden tools and the lawnmower locked away out of your child's reach.

Safe Outings

When you take your child to the park or playground, let her be as free as possible but keep an eye on her and look out for any hazards. Don't let your child walk near other children swinging, watch her when she goes on the slide and help her on the climbing frame. Keep her away from dog droppings and don't let her go up and hug dogs she doesn't know. Sadly, it is the case that you must not leave your child unattended at any time in the park or playground. If you take your child swimming, do not let her walk around the pool unattended and always make sure she has armbands or a float-suit.

When you're out in town or shopping, again be aware of hazards such as escalators, heavy swing doors and lifts. If your child is not in the buggy, reins are a good idea as they help to prevent him falling or running into the road. You need to teach your child road sense from an early age, so talk to him about stopping, looking and listening, and waiting for the green signal at pedestrian crossings. Teach your child not to pick up rubbish, and always have some wet-wipes to hand in case he does pick up anything dirty.

Sun Safety

In hot weather, it is important that you use a good sunblock for your child and don't leave her sitting in direct sun, as children can overheat very quickly. If she is in her buggy use a sunshade or push her into the shade. Don't sit with your child in the midday sun in the summer when the sun is at its hottest. Make sure your child plays in the shade; have picnics in the shade if the weather is very hot. Make sure your child has a high-factor sunscreen on (factor 50 or more), and is wearing a long-sleeved shirt and a sun hat if she is going to be exposed to the sun for a while. As Australians say, 'Slip on a shirt, slop on some sunscreen and slap on a hat!'

If your child has been exposed to hot sun without any protection he may well have sunburn. His skin will be red and hot to the touch, and he will be very uncomfortable. Take any tight layers of clothing off, and cool his skin with tepid water. Give him plenty to drink as well. For mild sunburn you can use a good aftersun cream, calamine lotion or aloe vera, which is especially soothing. If you are going outdoors, keep his skin covered with loose long-sleeved clothes and plenty of high-factor sunblock. Sunburn often takes a few days to settle down, and your child's skin may peel before it heals properly. If your child's skin blisters then it is a good idea to seek medical advice.

If you have been out on a hot day and your child hasn't spent much time in the shade, she can develop sunstroke. If she has sunstroke she will be very hot one minute and cold and shivery the next. She may feel sick and have a headache, and she will be very miserable. Her temperature may be raised as well. You need to bring her in out of the sun into a cool room and give her plenty of cool drinks. Give paracetamol to reduce her temperature and help with any pain. Make sure she doesn't go back into the sun for any length of time over the next day or so. If your child has a very high temperature and appears lethargic and unwell, then take her to the hospital or to your doctor.

Car Safety

When travelling in the car, you will need a car seat or booster seat, depending on your child's height. Always strap your child securely into the car seat. Once your child can reach the door handles, you'll need to lock the child safety locks on the passenger doors. Don't leave your child unattended by the car when you park or move the car in or out of the garage.

Closing Thoughts

It's important to be vigilant in thinking about your child's safety, but remember there's a balance to be struck. There is no such thing as the perfect parent, and accidents will happen. Try to be as relaxed as you can when caring for your child and don't be consumed with worry. Children do not need to be mollycoddled, and they need the freedom of being exposed to some risks, as that is part of growing up. If children are always overprotected, they can grow up fearful of life and new experiences and not want to join in rough-and-tumble play with others.

CHAPTER 10

Childhood Illnesses

You may have got to the end of your child's first year of life without him having any illnesses at all, and this is more common if he is your first baby. However, most one-year-olds have had the occasional cough or raised temperature but probably not much more. During the toddler years it is likely that your child will pick up more infections, as he is mixing with other children more, and he may suffer from one of the common infectious diseases such as chickenpox. None of us wants our child to be ill, and when this happens we want to make him better as soon as we can. However, most illnesses in the toddler years come and go very quickly, and although your child may seem very unwell, within a few days he will usually bounce back and be full of energy again.

As a parent, you'll probably have quite a strong intuition about your child not being well, and in the days before an infection appears you may sense that she's not herself. Often the first signs of illness are that she doesn't want to eat and sleeps more than usual. She may be hot and sticky or complain that she hurts but doesn't really know where. A raised temperature often accompanies infections in children, but can usually be easily treated with infant paracetamol or ibuprofen and plenty of fluids.

I must stress at the beginning that you should seek medical advice if you are at all concerned about your child's health, as this chapter is not intended to replace such advice.

Treating and Preventing Common Illnesses

It is a good idea to have a medicine box or a locked cupboard containing the medicines you need to treat common symptoms of illnesses so that you're not dashing around in the night trying to find the Calpol. It's also a good idea to have a portable first aid kit for scrapes and injuries to use when you're out and about. A basic first aid kit should contain:

- *infant paracetamol suspension such as Calpol*
- *antiseptic cream or witch hazel*
- *antihistamine cream for bites and stings*
- *skin-soothing cream such as Sudocrem*
- *high-factor suncream (factor 50 or more)*
- *antiseptic wipes*
- *plasters*
- *cotton wool*
- *round-ended scissors*
- *tweezers*
- *crepe bandages.*

The Medicine Cabinet

I've listed here the basic things you will need to treat children's illnesses, which it's worth keeping a stock of in your medicine cabinet.

- *plastic syringe or spoon for measuring doses of medicine*
- *thermometer*
- *infant paracetamol suspension*
- *ibuprofen suspension suitable for children*
- *antihistamine such as Piriton (the liquid form is suitable for children)*
- *cough medicine suitable for children*
- *decongestant rub such as Vicks Vaporub*
- *rehydration sachets such as Dioralyte*
- *antihistamine cream for bites and stings*
- *witch hazel for bumps and bruises*
- *antiseptic cream*
- *nappy-rash cream such as Sudocrem for sore bottoms*
- *high-factor suncream (factor 50 or more)*
- *moisturizing or emollient cream for dry skin*
- *plasters, bandages and cotton wool*
- *scissors, tweezers and nail clippers.*

Alternative Medicines

Many people today are turning to alternative medicines, and of course a lot of these remedies have been used for centuries and work well. Skin treatments made from natural products work particularly well, such as calendula or camomile for soothing rashes, witch hazel or tea tree oil as natural antiseptics, and arnica as an anti-inflammatory and for treating bruises. However, often alternative medicines can take longer to work than conventional medicine, and I feel that where children are concerned it is important that you relieve their pain or discomfort as soon as possible.

If you are keen to use alternative medicine for your child then it's important to find a registered practitioner to talk to, and also find out information about such treatment from your doctor or a medical helpline such as NHS Direct in the UK.

Immunizations

There has been much discussion in the media recently of the possible 'risks' of immunization, particularly the MMR (measles, mumps and rubella) vaccination given when children are around one. Much of this concern has proved unfounded: there is no proven link between MMR and autism. Personally, I always advise parents to go ahead with the immunizations that are offered for their child, but you as parents must make this choice. I believe that infectious diseases such as measles are far worse than any side effects from the immunization, and most parents want to protect their child from serious infectious diseases. The important thing is to talk to health professionals about it so that you can make your mind up and feel easy about it.

When you take your child for immunization appointments, it's important that he doesn't have a cold or other infection and is feeling well, otherwise the vaccination can make him feel very unwell. Most children will feel quite grumpy and tired the evening after the vaccination and may be under the weather for a day or two. It's a good idea to give a dose of paracetamol or ibuprofen before bed after vaccinations to help with any discomfort or fever.

Raised Temperature

Your child's normal temperature should be between 36 and 37°C (97 and 99°F) but will commonly go up to around 39°C (102°F) when she has an infection. If your child's temperature does not reduce within 24 hours of taking medication or is over 40°C (104°F), you need to call your general practitioner. If your child has a raised temperature, you need to give her paracetamol or ibuprofen suspension on a regular basis. Also ensure that she has plenty of fluids such as water or diluted juice to drink. If her skin is very hot due to a high temperature, you can use a cool flannel for her face and take off layers of clothes to keep her comfortable.

Febrile Convulsions

Young children sometimes have a fit or seizure (convulsion) when they have a high temperature. This is caused by a sharp rise in body temperature due to an infection. If your child has a febrile convulsion he will shake and move his arms and legs around in a jerky way, and may lose consciousness for a few moments. Most febrile convulsions last less than a minute, but they can last up to five minutes. This can be very frightening for you as a parent, but your child will usually make a full recovery quickly. Lay him on his side and sit with him to reassure him. When the fit has passed he may be very tired and just want to sleep. It's a good idea to give him paracetamol or ibuprofen to bring his temperature down. If this is the first convulsion your child has had, call the doctor, who will probably want to see your child just to check him over. If a convulsion lasts more than five minutes or if you are concerned, call an ambulance straight away to get medical attention for your child.

Infectious Diseases

Chickenpox

The first sign of chickenpox is usually a small red spot on your child's face or torso. Within two to three days more spots will appear and begin to fill up with fluid and look like blisters. Your child will often be covered all over her body, and she can get spots in her mouth and ears and under her eyelids. Once the spots have blistered, they become very itchy and your child will probably have a temperature and feel quite unwell. The best way to treat chickenpox is with infant paracetamol or ibuprofen given regularly to reduce fever, an antihistamine medicine such as Piriton to reduce itching, and calamine lotion to soothe the skin. It's a good idea to keep your child's nails short and clean so that she doesn't damage her skin if she scratches the spots. Make sure your child has plenty to drink, and you will probably find she has little appetite and wants to sleep.

Chickenpox is caught through direct contact with other infected children, but unfortunately a child can be infectious on the day before the spots first appear. Once exposed to the infection, it can take 10 to 21 days for chickenpox to appear. The disease continues to be very infectious until all the spots have scabbed over, so you need to avoid taking your child where he could infect other children during this time unless you have checked with the other parents that their children have already had chickenpox.

Measles

Measles is vaccinated against nowadays with the MMR immunization, and it is a very nasty disease for your child to get if he is not immunized. The first symptoms of measles are usually sneezing, runny eyes and swollen eyelids and a slightly raised temperature. After a few days a spotty rash appears, usually beginning around the ears and neck and spreading across the face and body. A child with measles will feel very ill, lethargic and achey, often with earache. If you suspect your child has measles, you need to contact your doctor, who will be able to confirm whether he has it. If your child does have measles, treat the fever and pain with paracetamol suspension or ibuprofen on a regular basis. Keep your child's eyes clean with cooled boiled water and cotton wool and let him lie in a darkened room, as his eyes will be very sensitive. Give plenty of fluids such as water or diluted fruit juice and don't worry if he is not hungry.

Measles is caught by contact with other infected children, often through sneezing and coughing. Children with measles are infectious about two to four days before the rash appears and for around five days afterwards, so it's advised that you keep your child away from others during this period. If your child has not been immunized and comes into contact with an infected child, it can take up to 21 days for the symptoms to appear.

Mumps

Mumps is vaccinated against as part of the MMR so it is rare nowadays, but it is a serious illness with a number of possible complications, especially for older children who are not immunized. One of the first signs of mumps is a large, noticeable swelling in the neck, which can be on one or both sides. This swelling usually lasts around four to eight days. A child with mumps will have a sore throat, earache and a headache, and may have a fever. Treat the pain and fever with paracetamol or ibuprofen suspension regularly, give plenty of fluids, and use a warm flannel to soothe the sore glands in the neck.

Mumps is caught through direct contact with infected children. A child with mumps is infectious from about a week before the neck glands swell until about five days after the swelling goes down. If your child is not immunized and comes into contact with mumps, it can take up to 21 days for the symptoms to appear.

Rubella

Rubella (also known as German measles) is vaccinated against as part of the MMR, and although it is a mild disease in children it can cause serious birth defects in unborn babies if their mothers catch rubella. The first signs of rubella are a brownish-red spotty rash around the neck, ears and torso. A child with rubella may have a fever and will have inflamed glands at the back of the neck and behind the ears. This swelling usually lasts about a week. Some children get quite ill with rubella, but in others you would hardly know they had it. If your child has a fever with rubella, treat with paracetamol or ibuprofen and make sure she has plenty of rest and fluids.

Rubella is caught through direct contact, and the most important thing if your child is infected is to make sure that you keep him away from anyone who is pregnant. If your child has been in contact with rubella it can take up to 21 days for symptoms to appear.

Scarlet Fever

Scarlet fever is an uncommon disease nowadays due to the use of antibiotics, but children can become infected with this illness, sometimes after having had chickenpox. Early signs of scarlet fever are a sore throat and a raised temperature, followed by a reddish rash over the body that feels rough to the touch. A child with scarlet fever will often also have a white coating on the tongue, which can peel and leave the tongue looking red and swollen (sometimes called a 'strawberry tongue'). If you suspect your child has scarlet fever then take her to your doctor, as she will need a course of antibiotics. Like any fever, scarlet fever can be treated with infant paracetamol or ibuprofen, and plenty of fluids.

Scarlet fever is caught through direct contact, but is unusual in children under two years of age. Symptoms usually appear within two to four days and the rash usually lasts around a week, although the skin can peel for quite a few weeks after the rash has faded.

'Slapped Cheek' Syndrome

'Slapped cheek' syndrome is a viral infection that is quite common in young children. A child with 'slapped cheek' will have cold- and flu-like symptoms and be generally tired and under the weather, and later in the infection a characteristic red rash will appear on the cheeks. Unfortunately, a child will be infectious before the rash appears, which is why there are often outbreaks of the infection in nurseries and schools. Paracetamol or ibuprofen can be given to reduce fever, and you should give your child plenty of fluids. This infection can be dangerous to unborn babies, especially in the first 20 weeks of pregnancy, so if you know your child has 'slapped cheek' make sure he does not come into contact with anyone who is pregnant.

Meningitis

Meningitis is a serious infection of the membrane surrounding the brain. Meningitis can be caused by bacteria, in which case the infection is more serious, or by a virus, which is a less serious illness. In recent years, the national vaccination programme for children in the UK has included vaccination against certain types of bacterial meningitis. The symptoms of meningitis can be quite difficult to spot and the infection progresses very quickly in young children, so if you suspect meningitis seek medical advice immediately. The early symptoms of meningitis are lethargy and drowsiness, sensitivity to light, vomiting and abnormal skin colour. A rash can appear with meningitis as a sign of blood poisoning (septicaemia), but it's important not to wait for a rash if you suspect that your child has meningitis. If your child has bacterial meningitis, she will probably need to be treated in hospital with antibiotics.

Chest Infections

Coughs and Colds

If your child has a cold he will have a runny nose, sneeze a lot and probably be rather miserable for a day or so. He may also have a mild chest infection and so may run a slightly raised temperature as well. He may develop a cough, which can disturb him at night. Infant paracetamol or ibuprofen can be given to ease any discomfort, bring down his temperature and help your child to sleep better. Use a good decongestant rub, and maybe have a vaporizer in his bedroom at night or put a vapour capsule on his pillow if he is in a bed. These all help to unblock your child's nose and so help him to breathe more easily. You'll probably find that your child doesn't want to eat much while he has a cold, so make sure he has plenty to drink. If you are worried that a cold does not seem to be clearing up or if your child is really unwell, get advice from your doctor or a medical helpline.

Croup

Croup is a harsh, rasping, wheezy cough caused by an infection of the chest, or less commonly the epiglottis (the valve in the throat shutting off the windpipe). If your child has croup she will sound hoarse and seem to struggle to get her breath. Often this starts at night and it can be very distressing for you and your child. To treat croup, sit her on your lap in a steamy bathroom and run the hot tap into the bath to create steam. This helps to ease the inflammation in her throat. A vaporizer in the bedroom can also help her breathing at night. Give her plenty to drink, including warm drinks to soothe her throat. If her skin changes colour and she is struggling to breathe or seems to deteriorate, then contact your doctor.

Bronchiolitis

Bronchiolitis is a chest infection that is common in children under two years old, and it usually happens in the colder months, between October and March. A child with bronchiolitis will have a blocked or runny nose, a cough and a tight chest and shallow breathing. The symptoms are usually mild at first, and then after a few days your child can seem very unwell and lethargic and his breathing will be laboured. It is important to see your doctor and get your child checked. If your child deteriorates rapidly or his skin changes colour you need to get urgent medical attention, either at a hospital or by phoning your doctor.

Ear, Nose and Throat Infections

Ear Infections

Ear infections are quite common in young children, and often the first sign is that your child's ear is red and she rubs or pulls it. If she has an inner-ear infection, she is likely to have a temperature and feel quite tired and under the weather. Fluid can build up behind the eardrum, which can burst, causing quite a lot of pain. Give your child painkillers such as infant paracetamol or ibuprofen to ease the pain of an ear infection. If you think your child has an ear infection it is best to go to your doctor, who can prescribe a cream for treating outer-ear infections or antibiotics for a bacterial inner-ear infection.

Glue Ear

Glue ear is a very common ear infection in children, which can go unnoticed as it may not cause any pain. Often the first signs that your child has glue ear are that he doesn't seem to be hearing you at times, his balance is a bit 'off' or he seems to be lagging behind with his speech development. If you are concerned about your child's hearing, it's a good idea to talk to your health visitor or doctor, who can refer your child for a hearing test. If your child does have glue ear, health professionals will usually suggest that you wait for around three months and have another hearing test to see if the infection has cleared up. If glue ear persists you will be referred to an ear, nose and throat specialist, who may recommend inserting a grommet (a small valve) into your child's ear and/or removing his adenoids.

Tonsillitis

If your child has tonsillitis she will have a sore throat, swollen tonsils and a high temperature and will feel really quite miserable. She may also have earache. She will not want to eat, and will probably want to cuddle up with you and just go to sleep. If you suspect your child has tonsillitis, get her to stick out her tongue so you can see her tonsils. If they are red and swollen and have white lumps on them, take her to see your doctor. Give your child plenty of fluids and keep her warm, and treat pain and fever with infant paracetamol or ibuprofen. She may also need a course of antibiotics. Unfortunately, some children seem to be especially prone to tonsillitis and get many bouts of this infection during their childhood.

Conjunctivitis

Conjunctivitis is an infection of the eyes, which can be caused by a virus or bacteria. If your child has conjunctivitis he will have a red eye, which may be runny and itchy, with a crust on his eyelid in the morning. This is very contagious and is likely to pass to his other eye too. Children can easily pass infective conjunctivitis to each other. You can soothe your child's eyes with cool water and clean them with tepid water on cotton wool. You do, however, need to see your doctor, who will usually prescribe some eye drops. Once treated, conjunctivitis should clear up quite quickly.

Gastric Problems

Vomiting

The most common cause of vomiting (being sick) in young children is infection. If your child has a viral or bacterial infection she will probably be sick and have diarrhoea, although the two don't always go together. Children often pick up stomach bugs through contact with others at nursery, or from older siblings if there is an infection going round at school. If you know there has been an outbreak of a gastric infection at your child's nursery or playgroup, take special care that she washes her hands (with antibacterial soap if possible) before eating and after using the potty.

If your child is vomiting, make sure he has plenty of fluids – no milk, just water and then very weak juice when he stops being sick. When he is feeling better let him have some plain food such as toast or crackers until you are sure he is not going to be sick again. Children will often feel quite hungry after having an upset stomach, but when you give them something to eat they may just have a little bit and not fancy any more. Let your child's appetite come back naturally and don't force him to eat big meals again; just make sure that he has small snacks when he feels like it. Once he is fully recovered, you will probably find that his appetite comes back with a vengeance. If vomiting continues for more than a day, call your doctor, as young children can dehydrate very quickly and this can cause them to deteriorate quite fast.

Diarrhoea

Again, the most common cause of diarrhoea is infection, passed on through either contaminated food or contact with other children. If your child has diarrhoea she will have very smelly, runny poo and she may also have stomach cramps. Sometimes toddlers develop mild diarrhoea after eating certain foods such as citrus fruit; however, this usually clears up on its own within a couple of days. You might also find that your child has quite loose, runny poo when she is teething. Older children who have been potty-trained may be quite distressed if they have diarrhoea and soil their pants, so it's important for you to be calm and reassuring and clean them up with minimal fuss.

To treat diarrhoea, make sure that your child has plenty of fluids to drink, especially water or diluted fruit juice. If you are breast- or bottle-feeding, you do not need to stop giving milk feeds, but you can make sure that your child has sips of water or diluted juice as well. If your child shows signs of dehydration such as being drowsy, not weeing very much or having very few wet nappies, then contact your doctor as soon as possible. He may prescribe rehydration drinks, which provide the right balance of salts, sugars and water to treat dehydration. Once your child feels like eating again, let him have a light diet of soups or plain starchy foods such as toast or potato.

Constipation

Constipation is when a child wants to do a poo but cannot, as it is so solid that it hurts her to pass it. If she does a poo it will be quite small and solid. This can then make your child anxious so that she 'holds on' to poo, which can become a vicious circle. Toddlers often go through phases of mild constipation when they are growing up, especially if they are eating less or refusing certain foods. If this happens to your child, don't worry, as it is not serious and will pass. Some children only do a poo every two or three days, and this does not necessarily mean that they are constipated. Keep an eye on your child's usual frequency of doing a poo;

if this becomes less regular she may be getting constipated.

To treat constipation, make sure that your child is having a good, balanced diet with plenty of fibre, fruit and vegetables and of course lots to drink. Fruits that are good to help constipation are apples and pears, and dried fruits such as prunes, apricots and figs. If your child won't eat these you could try giving them in the form of juice to drink. If your child has become frightened about doing a poo a good way to help is to let him blow up a balloon while sitting on the toilet. The action of blowing helps him to bear down, which sometimes encourages a bowel movement, so this is worth trying.

Urinary Infections

Girls are more susceptible to urinary tract infections than boys because the urethra (the tube that passes urine from the bladder out of the body) is shorter in girls and closer to the anus, and bacteria can travel up it more easily. If your child has a urinary tract infection she may have pain when doing a wee and want to wee more often. The urine may be a darker colour and have a slight smell and you may see blood in the urine. She may have a raised temperature too, particularly if she has a kidney infection; this will require medical treatment.

If your child has a urinary infection, make sure she has plenty of fluids. Cranberry juice seems to be particularly good for treating infection of the bladder (cystitis). However, if symptoms persist, take your child to your doctor, who can prescribe antibiotics.

Skin Conditions

Nappy Rash

Nappy rash is most common in younger toddlers who haven't been potty-trained, but children can still develop sore bottoms during potty-training if they have accidents and are left in wet pants. Nappy rash is caused by irritation of the delicate skin on your child's bottom, either because of contact with wee and poo or infection. Teething can also make your child more susceptible to nappy rash. The rash can vary from a mild spotty redness to a very painful, blistered rash due to infection.

Prevention is always better than cure, so use a good barrier cream regularly on your child's bottom, especially at the first sign of soreness.

Clean your child's bottom carefully with warm water and give him plenty of time without nappies or pants on to encourage healing. If your child has a very sore infected rash, see your doctor, who can prescribe a steroid cream or antibiotics to treat infection. Nappy rash can also be a symptom of thrush, which is caused by a fungus, in which case you can be prescribed an antifungal cream.

Cradle Cap

Cradle cap is scaly, yellowish patches on your child's scalp, which can develop at any time. It is caused by the build-up of dead skin and is nothing to worry about, as it is easy to treat at home. Put baby oil or olive oil on some cotton wool and rub it gently into your child's scalp – this can be tricky if she has a very full head of hair! Rub the oil onto the patches of cradle cap with circular movements and leave it on overnight if you can. Wash out the next day with a gentle shampoo. You may have to do this for several days until it is all treated. Don't pick it off, as the scalp can become infected, but comb it out gently. You will usually find that the oil has a softening effect and it comes off easily.

Eczema

Many children develop eczema in the early months of their lives, which can be very painful and debilitating if left untreated. It can cause bad irritation at night and a young child can suffer from disturbed sleep because of it. It may be hereditary or an allergic reaction to certain foods, dust or animal hair. If your child has eczema you will notice patches of dry skin in the folds of his arms, knees, hands and wrists, which will develop into an itchy reddish rash. It is a good idea to take him to your doctor to confirm that it is eczema. You may be prescribed an emollient such as aqueous cream or a bath oil such as Oilatum. Make sure you use a non-biological washing powder and avoid woollen clothes next to his skin. If your child's eczema is very bad he may need to have cream all over his body at night and wear an all-in-one sleepsuit with mittens to prevent him from scratching.

Allergies

Asthma

Asthma is an increasingly common condition in children nowadays. A child can develop asthma in the early toddler years, especially if there is a family history of it. There also seems to be a genetic link between asthma, eczema and hay fever. If your child has asthma you will notice she has a nasty rasping cough, finding it difficult to get her breath. She may also have a tight chest and feel generally under the weather. This can be worse at night or when your child is running around and active. A severe asthma attack will cause your child to struggle hard to breathe, and her skin may change colour. In the case of a severe attack you must get medical help as soon as possible.

The most common treatment for asthma is an inhaler. Your general practitioner can prescribe this and talk to you about the different types of inhalers. They bring quick relief of asthma symptoms, helping your child to breathe more easily.

Hay Fever

Young children can be susceptible to hay fever in the same way as adults, and it can be very distressing for them. If your child suffers from hay fever he will have a runny nose and eyes, and will sneeze a lot during the season when the pollen count is high. Take him to your doctor, who can prescribe you something to help, such as an infant antihistamine. Your child might seem quite lethargic and tired if he has a bad attack of hay fever and unfortunately antihistamines can also make him drowsy.

Food Allergies

Some children can be allergic to certain foods, such as nuts. Your child may complain of tingling in her lips, there may be swelling of her lips or tongue and she may also be wheezing. If she is struggling to breathe, ring the emergency services. If your child is otherwise well but feels tingling or swelling in her lips or tongue, arrange to see your doctor.

Common Childhood Injuries

Burns and Scalds

Once your child is a toddler and running round it is much more likely for accidents to happen, and unfortunately the risk of burns and scalds increases during this time. As far as possible, keep your child away from hot liquids, the kettle and hot appliances in the home (see the section on safety at home in Chapter 9). To treat a burn or scald, run cool or tepid water over the area for at least 15 to 20 minutes. Do not apply ice, butter or ointments, as this could trap the heat under the skin. If the area of skin burned or scalded is large, you need to immerse the area in cool water, but make sure to keep your child warm. Once the burn or scald is cooled cover the skin with clingfilm or a clear plastic bag and seek medical advice, either at a hospital or your local doctor's surgery.

Cuts and Grazes

Once your child has learnt to walk he will very likely have lots of tumbles and endless cuts and grazes on his knees. Clean these gently with water and cotton wool and put on some antiseptic cream, such as Savlon, to prevent infection and to aid healing. It is usually best to keep the wound open to the air as this will help the healing process. If he is bleeding a lot you may need to put a plaster on. Most minor cuts and grazes heal within a few days, but if your child is bleeding badly and you cannot stop it by putting pressure on the wound then it's probably best to seek medical attention.

Many children cut their lips when they fall over and they bleed quite a lot for what seems to be several minutes. Normally this heals on its own; it is just very sore for a few hours. Make sure the wound is clean, and put an ice cube on if it doesn't stop bleeding.

If your child has a bruise from a fall and the skin is not broken then you can use witch hazel. This is a natural remedy that you can buy at the chemist. I always had a bottle in the cupboard when our children were growing up, and just getting the bottle out would make them feel better straight away.

Choking

Once your child is a toddler she will probably be feeding herself a lot of the time, and certainly with finger food. Some toddlers often stuff so much in their mouths that they start to choke. Toddlers can also choke on small toys or objects if they put them in their mouths. This can be very frightening for both you and your child. If she does choke, then open her mouth and try to get the food or object out by putting a finger and thumb in and sweeping it out if you can. If it is wedged in, lean her forward, supporting her chest with your hand, and give her a good sharp tap between the shoulder blades with the heel of your hand. This normally works and you find the food or object comes flying out, much to the relief of everyone! If you cannot dislodge what your child is choking on and she is struggling to breathe you must call the emergency services.

Bites and Stings

Stings from insects, such as bees, wasps and mosquitoes, can be very painful for your child. If your child has been bitten he will have a red mark and an itchy raised swelling on his skin. If a bee has stung your child you may see the sting still in his skin; you can carefully remove this with tweezers. Soothe his skin with antihistamine cream or give him an antihistamine medicine such as Piriton. If your child has been stung in his mouth or throat and it begins to swell, take him straight to a hospital, because once the area swells up it will affect his breathing.

If your child has been bitten by a dog or cat you may well be able to treat it at home by cleaning the wound and putting on some antiseptic cream and a dressing. If your child has been badly bitten take her straight to the hospital.

Staying in Hospital

There may be a time when your child needs to go into hospital and stay overnight. This can be very unsettling for everyone in the family, especially your child. Many hospitals have facilities where a parent can stay at night and be with their child. If you have someone to care for your other children, then I would recommend that you stay with your child if you can. If your child is old enough, explain that Mummy or Daddy is coming too and that hospital is where we go sometimes when we are not very well. Tell him that the doctors and nurses are very kind and will look after you both while you're there. Talking like this may help you too if you feel a bit uneasy about hospitals or nervous about the treatment your child is having. If you have time, make sure to pack some of his favourite toys, books and games. Take his special cuddly toy that he has at bedtime and anything that he is very attached too. A CD player is good so that he can listen to his favourite music.

If you are facing a long stay in hospital with your child, it is important that a family member or friend comes and takes over from you from time to time. When your child comes home you may find that her behaviour is affected; she may be quite clingy or revert to babyish behaviour. She has probably had more attention from you and others than before and so it's an adjustment coming home. Be patient with this and you will find that she settles down again gradually and family life returns to normal.

CHAPTER 11

Having Another Baby

Many parents have commented on what a shock it is to family life having another baby, particularly the second, and have asked me to write a chapter dedicated to this. I think if you have another baby quite soon after your first, particularly if it is not planned, it can seem a huge amount of work, and you wonder how you can possibly divide your time between the two children. However, don't despair; you will adjust and there will be much enjoyment in seeing your older child beginning to love and play with his baby brother or sister.

Deciding to Have Another Baby

Having another baby is a personal decision for you and your partner, and it is a good idea to talk it through together. When my husband and I were having our family, it was quite usual to have a three-year gap between children, whereas nowadays it seems that many families are having their children closer together. Remember that there is no perfect age gap, and much depends on your family circumstances. There are advantages in small age gaps, as your children will probably play well together as they grow up, and you may not need to have a long career break. Many families who have several children close together have a real sense of fulfilment in seeing their children growing up as firm friends and being able to move on to the next stages in life after having young children. The disadvantages are that you will be very busy during the preschool years, and the babycare can seem never-ending. Tiredness can be overwhelming, and there may not seem to be very much else in life apart from the day-to-day business of looking after children. With larger age gaps between children, the advantages are that you will probably enjoy pregnancy more and be able to rest more when the babies are born, and the older siblings will be able to help you with babycare. Older children are better able to understand and eagerly anticipate a new baby, and will probably adore the baby when he or she comes along. I had a six-year gap between my second and third child and the older two were very excited about the baby coming and just wanted to help. The other side of the coin, however, is that your child-rearing days will go on for longer. You will also find that you have to juggle school runs and after-school activities with babycare and toddler groups.

So how do you manage if you haven't planned another baby and find you are pregnant again before you feel ready? Often second and subsequent babies just happen, and for some mothers it can take quite a while for the reality to sink in. You may feel you have only just got your body back after giving birth. You also may still be breast-feeding, and the thought of having another baby may fill you with horror. In my experience, however, the reality is that once the baby comes along you do adjust and the addition to the family becomes a joy – in fact, you can't imagine life without her. On the other hand, if you had been trying for a baby for some time before you conceived your first, you will probably be delighted that you are pregnant again.

Coping with Pregnancy and Birth

When you find out that you are pregnant again you will discover that you probably won't be able to rest as much as you did when you were expecting your first child. You will find that you tire more quickly whether you are working or at home with your toddler. Often those first few weeks can seem endless, especially if you suffer from morning sickness. If this is the case, make sure you have family or friends to help out when you need them, particularly in the early weeks and then later on in your pregnancy when you get heavy and tired. A good idea is to have a nap when your toddler naps, as he will be very active, particularly if he is walking, and will keep you on your toes when he is awake. Keep active, though, and go out for walks and take gentle exercise unless your doctor has told you not to. Also a good diet is important, as you will be dashing around with a toddler and burning up lots of energy.

Usually first babies are born in hospital but sometimes second and subsequent babies are born at home, particularly if the first delivery was straightforward. I would have loved to have had my babies at home but it wasn't the 'done thing' in those days. When Jayne (my third child) was born we lived 25 miles (40 km) from the hospital that I would have gone to had I needed medical intervention, so home birth wasn't an option. My own mother had the first four of us at home and the last two were born in hospital. My parents employed a maternity nurse who lived in and delivered the baby and then stayed on for a month to help my mother.

It seems to be more popular now to be able to have your baby at home, and I think it is a lovely thing to do if you think it will work for you. There is something very special about having your baby at home, but you really will need help afterwards. If you are going to have a home birth it is a good idea to make sure grandparents or close friends look after your toddler while you are in labour, as it is unlikely you will want to worry about her while giving birth! Of course this applies if you are having a hospital delivery too. Make sure you have some help on hand after the baby is born too, as it is not like having a first child, when you can feed the baby and go back to bed. You will need to rest after the baby is born. It really does pay off if you can rest, so help is necessary. It is good if your partner can take some time off work as he can help with your toddler and of course get to know the baby; this can be a very precious time. It also enables him to have some rest and catch up on sleep.

What Kind of Help Do I Need?

Lots of families ask parents or relations to help out after a new baby is born. If you are on good terms with your family then this can work very well. Grandparents will often be delighted to be asked and very happy to get involved. Not all grandparents will want to be up at night, though, so remember this and instead let them do the running around with your toddler. If you are having twins or triplets then you really will need help, so get it organized well before your babies are due to be born.

What other help can you have if your family is unable to be with you and your partner has to work? Depending on your finances, there are several options. Having a maternity nurse come to live in and help with the baby is one way to do it, but she won't look after your toddler too; she will only look after you and your baby and cover the nights for you. This of course means that you get plenty of rest when you need it. You could have a maternity nurse just come in at night and look after the baby and feed him. This would mean that you are on your own during the day, which of course some people prefer. Employing a maternity nurse is quite costly, but many people say to me that it is the best money they have spent, as it enables the mother to rest and means you have someone to teach you what to do and help with the baby. Sometimes grandparents will pay for a maternity nurse to come to live in for just a week or two; this can also be a great help. It is worth thinking about this option if you can manage it financially.

What other help can you get? You could use a doula (non-medical caregiver), who will be with you during the birth and then stay on afterwards for a week or so to do the household chores. This option can be a great help and is becoming quite popular. Some people employ a nanny, who will look after the toddler and help round the house. This again is quite costly but well worth it if you find a good, helpful nanny.

Employing an au pair can work well. Remember, though, that au pairs are young girls who often have very little experience of family life with children and also may be homesick. You do not want to be dealing with this when you have just had a baby. If you are going to employ an au pair make sure you take her on well before the baby is due, to give yourselves time to get to know her and also for her to settle into life with you. I have worked alongside some lovely au pairs who were very keen to learn about babies and young children. If she has not had experience with young children you should not leave your toddler with her on her own until you feel confident that she would cope in a crisis. It is not fair on her to do this if she is not experienced.

Preparing Your Toddler for a Sibling

I don't think there is any hard and fast rule about when to tell your toddler he is going to have a baby brother or sister. I think, though, that if your child is between twelve and twenty-four months old it can seem an awfully long time to wait if you tell him in the early days of your pregnancy. Of course if you are feeling very unwell and not coping, it may be a good idea to say 'Mummy isn't well because she has a baby in her tummy' and leave it at that. You may find that a young child will forget all about it, as he has lots of other things going on in his life. When another baby is on the way you may feel you want your toddler to know, and if you do decide to tell him it can be exciting as he can feel your tummy and feel the baby kicking. Some parents don't tell their todddler until the new baby is moving around and Mummy has quite a bump. On the other hand, you can explain to an older child why you're not feeling well and take him along to scans, and let him feel your tummy as the baby grows. There are lots of books for children about the experience of having a new baby brother or sister, which can help to make it seem more real to your child. When to tell your child or children really does depend on how old they are, and is a very personal decision.

It is a good idea not to move your toddler out of the nursery into another bedroom or put her in a bed at the same time as you have a new baby. Lots of parents ask me if there is a 'right time' to move their toddler, either from the nursery into her own room or out of her cot. If your child is two years old or under and is happy in her cot then I would leave her in it until she is a little older and things with the baby have settled down. If your child is over two years of age and you feel it is time she went into a bed, then try to make the change two to three months before the baby is due to be born. This gives her lots of time to settle into her bed and maybe a new bedroom too. She can help you put the cot away for the new baby, and you can tell her she is a grown-up girl now.

The space you have in your house will determine whether you move your toddler out of the nursery into his own room; he may be in his own room already and not need to move. If you have to move him make sure you do it well before the baby comes so that he is used to his new bedroom and doesn't think he has been pushed out because of a new baby. Many parents ask me if they can put a new baby in the same bedroom as a toddler. I would not do that straight away, as you will probably want to have the baby in with you for at least a week or so. They can go in together at some stage, but make sure that your toddler cannot and will not harm the baby in any way. If your toddler is still in a cot and can't get out or throw things into the baby's cot, then it would be fine to put them in together. If your toddler is in a bed then you need to judge whether it is safe to have the two children in together.

Dealing with Your Toddler's Reaction to the New Baby

I think every parent worries about how their toddler will react to having a new baby in the house. Having another sibling is part of family life and has been happening since time began, so try not to make too big an issue out of it. You will be amazed how soon a toddler will get used to a new baby in the house and she will soon forget the time when the baby wasn't there. New babies often get lots of presents and a toddler may feel a little left out, so a good idea is to buy a present and give it to your child 'from the baby' when he is born. You often find that this present becomes very special to your toddler.

There are lots of ways you can help your toddler to bond with the baby. The most important thing is to make them feel involved and encourage them to have a special role as a big brother or sister. Let him sit in an armchair and hold the baby in his arms, making sure you have an arm round them in case he decides to suddenly get up. Take photos of him holding the baby; this can make him feel very grown-up. Talk to him about what you are doing with the baby, asking him to do little errands for you by fetching nappies and things you need. He can be involved at bathtime, helping you to dry the baby when he comes out of the bath. He can also help you to get the baby dressed and ready for his feeds.

Some toddlers react strongly at feeding times, particularly if you are breast-feeding. You may find she wants to climb all over you, which can be very annoying when you want to concentrate on feeding the baby. If this happens then I suggest you let your toddler sit with you on the sofa and cuddle her while you feed the baby, but either give her some books to look at or put on a good children's DVD. Before I had a family I thought it would be the worst thing in the world to let a child watch a video or the television when you needed some peace, but I soon realized that for practical purposes when you have more than one child it is a very good idea and a great help. Be as relaxed as you can when feeding your new baby; you could try keeping a special basket of toys for your toddler just for feeding times. These can be very precious times of bonding for your child and your new baby. Lots of mums get very worried and feel guilty about not giving the new baby as much of their time as they did for their first baby. Try not to worry, though, as there will be other times in the day when your toddler is in bed and you can concentrate on the baby. As long as your baby is fed and clean he will not worry too much if you are not giving him your full concentration at some of his feeds.

The other thing that a toddler will very often do is start waking up in the night and screaming for no apparent reason. If your toddler is doing this, rest assured that it is very common. In nearly all the homes I have worked in with a toddler as well as a new baby, the toddler would wake at night at some stage, particularly if he was under about two and a half years of age. This is often linked to his mother having gone off to hospital and been away from home for maybe a couple of nights, and the huge change of having a new baby in the house. I have gone into detail about this in Chapter 4, but the main thing to remember is that your toddler is not being naughty but is adjusting to a huge change. He needs reassurance and cuddles before you settle him back to bed.

Another very common behaviour pattern when a new baby arrives is for your toddler to go off her food. She may just stop eating or her appetite may fall dramatically. Again, this is often a reaction to change, and it will pass. I have written about this in Chapter 5, but my usual advice is to not make too much fuss and to give her time to settle back into her normal appetite. You may also be surprised that your toddler tries to hit the baby or pokes him in his cot or pram. Sometimes this is because she is fascinated by the baby or, of course, because she is jealous. She may throw terrible temper tantrums; you may see behaviour that you have never seen before in her, or she may revert to very babyish behaviour. This is often partly because she is a toddler and partly because of the new baby in the house. I advise parents not to say things in front of a toddler such as 'She is being so naughty since the baby was born' or 'He just doesn't like the baby and wants him to go back.' This will not help you to sort out any difficult behaviour, as she will understand what you are saying. Try to say positive things in front of her to enable her to feel loved and secure, and remember that it is a huge adjustment for her now that she has to share you and your partner with the baby – she is coping with not being the only one any more.

Some children of just over a year are not at all interested in the new baby, especially if their life can go on much the same. They hardly seem to notice the baby but may still wake in the night, have tantrums or go off their food. This will be related to the fact that you are looking after a new baby. Whatever age your toddler or child is, remember that he too needs to feel part of this new family. I can remember as a child not being allowed to go to see my mother after a new baby was born, whether at home or in hospital, and I missed her very much and just wanted to be with her. So remember that your older child or children have quite strong feelings about being with you.

Dividing Your Time as Parents

As I have already said, most mothers often feel guilty about not spending more time with a new baby, as having a second baby is very different from a first and we have to learn how to divide our time between our children.

Try not to let it worry you, as it is all part of family life, and as long as children are loved and cared for they will not grow up with hang-ups if you haven't spent as much time with them in the early days as you would have liked. In fact, a second child can often be more secure and seem content to play on her own because she has learned to share your attention from the very beginning. It's also easy to feel guilty that your toddler is not getting as much of your time as she had before. However, this is a positive thing as it will help her to begin to learn to share and to wait for attention, which is an important part of growing up.

I can't emphasize enough the importance of dads, particularly when a new baby comes along. When your toddler is demanding Mum's attention and she can't give it, Dad can often step in and take him out to do special 'grown-up' things together. Dads often have a great capacity for energetic, rough-and-tumble play when Mum is exhausted, and this is just what toddlers need. Equally, Dad can take the baby out for walks in the pram, or take him to the shops so that your toddler can have some precious time with you. The most important thing is to talk to each other as parents and support each other in the challenges of being new parents again, and also of bringing up a toddler.

It can be a challenge to find time together as parents once you've had a second or subsequent child; however, it's still important to do this when you can. Weekends can be a good time to go out all together as a family, so that you don't feel one of you is spending all the time with the baby and one is dashing round with the toddler. On a practical note, it's worth thinking before you have another baby about how you'll transport a baby and a toddler when you are out for walks. You can either get a double buggy (the side-by-side models seem to be easier to push), or you can get a buggy board to clip onto the buggy so your toddler can stand by the handle and get pushed along.

It can be quite an adjustment to find you no longer have your evenings to yourselves because of feeding and waking in the night. It's a good idea to get your baby into a flexible routine (see *The Baby Book* for details) so that you can have some time between feeds for a glass of wine or a meal together. When you are able, make some time to go out or to be together alone; if you have family or close friends nearby, ask them to babysit now and again so that you can have some time to relax away from the children.

Closing Thoughts

However you go about integrating a new baby into family life, try to make it a fun time that you will look back on with great happiness. One of the most important things to remember is to include your toddler in all you do with the baby. Most parents find their toddler's behaviour is affected while they are going through the period of getting used to another little person in the home. If this is happening to you, try not to worry about it as your toddler will soon adjust and love her baby brother or sister and they will be the greatest of friends.

CHAPTER 12

Building a Strong Family Life

My hope for this chapter is that it will give you some clear, practical suggestions for building a strong family life. The chapter looks at how to enjoy your individual roles as a mum and a dad, as well as how to work together in your parenting. I feel that a sense of fun and happiness with plenty of laughter is important for family life. Parenting young children can be exhausting, but it is great fun, and children do and say such funny things as they are growing up that you can't help but laugh! Family time can be a great tonic, especially when you're feeling stressed out with the business of everyday life.

How to Enjoy Being a Mum

I believe that as a mother you need to take time out for yourself if you can, and not feel guilty about doing so. This will help you to enjoy motherhood more. I cannot stress enough how important this is, whether you stay at home with your child or go out to work, as either way being a mum can be exhausting at times. Often mums find the space to take time out from their first child, but it's just as vital when you have more than one child. The best thing to do is whatever gives you most pleasure. This could be having your hair done, having a manicure or a massage, meeting friends for coffee and having a good chat for an hour or so, or going to the cinema. If you have a good relationship with your own mother, it can be lovely to spend some time with her without the grandchildren. This often deepens your relationship as you share stories of what it's like to be a mother; she will benefit from this too. Try to find a friend or relative who can look after your child for a little while so that you can be free to go out. You may want to do something one evening a week, such as joining a gym, a painting class or whatever interests you. Evenings are often a good time to find a babysitter, or maybe your partner could babysit. Doing something somewhere where you're not 'just a mum' can be stimulating for your mind, and helps to refresh you and recharge your batteries for the demands of parenting young children.

As a mother, it helps to recognize the importance of what you're doing for your children. This applies whether you're a working mum or whether you're staying at home. A particular struggle for stay-at-home mums can be being asked the question, 'Do you work?' You may want to scream and say 'Of course I work, I am a full-time mum!' When life feels mundane, take some time out to think about all that your child is learning and the funny and lovely things he does, and maybe think about your hopes and dreams for him as he grows up. The toddler years pass quickly and you will probably find that you look back on them with great nostalgia – honestly! It can help you to value your role as a mum when you take time to just be with your child and get involved with whatever game he's playing. Don't feel you have to be constantly doing household jobs, as your child will love the moments when he has your undivided attention. In Chapter 7 there are lots of ideas for things you can do together with your toddler.

Mothers of toddlers often talk to me about how to balance being a mum with working either full- or part-time. Many people reading this book will be in this situation and will wonder at times how they will be able to keep going, faced with the demands of a toddler and a busy job. I understand these pressures and wish there was an easy answer. The most important thing is not to feel guilty. Many women feel they enjoy motherhood more once they have a couple of days a week back in the workplace, where they're not just 'Mummy'. On the other hand, some mothers find it a struggle to cope with the feelings of exhaustion and even guilt. I feel the most important thing is to get the childcare right so that when you are at work you are not worried about how your child is being cared for and whether she is happy. Grandparents are often very willing helpers with childcare, and can be brilliant at this. However, remember that looking after children can be exhausting, and try not to overload grandparents. It's worth having an honest discussion with grandparents before you set up childcare arrangements about how much they feel they can do and whether they would like any payment to be involved.

As a working mother it's still vitally important to make time for yourself, and not to feel that working time stands in for 'you time';

remember you're responding to demands at work just as much as when you're looking after your children. When you're a working mum, it's especially important to talk to your partner about how the domestic jobs will be shared out and to support one another as much as you can in housework and the childcare routines when you both get home.

It is a temptation to expect to be on the go all the time and to feel guilty if your child is not constantly entertained. There are now so many organized activities outside the home, even for toddlers, and I feel that sometimes it all gets out of hand and is too much for both you and your child. There can also be a sense of pressure to keep up with what other mothers are doing. Equally, at home many mums feel that they have to constantly provide new things for their child to do, rather than encouraging him to play on his own at times. It is perfectly all right for your child to be quietly at home with you playing with his toys while you have a sit-down with a coffee and the newspaper. Many mothers forget this, so remember that you need to have some quiet time too. If your child is still having a daytime nap then put your feet up while he is napping, at least for some of that time. If he is not napping and you are at home with him, take time out together after lunch. Put your feet up on the sofa and tuck him in with you with a book or a DVD, and tell him 'We are going to have a little rest now.' These times together can be very precious, and it's good to make the most of them before your child's day is busy with nursery or school.

Finally, one of the best things you can do to help you enjoy being a mum is to get to know and meet other parents. This can help you all share the load of looking after young children, and you could go to the park together, take your children for a good walk, or treat them to lunch or a snack out at a child-friendly cafe. Even the supermarket can be a lot easier when there's more than one adult around. This gives mothers time to talk together and encourage each other, and also gives your children time to spend together playing. If you're having a difficult time with your child or just going through toddler tantrums, it can be a good antidote to meet up with friends who have children, even if you only go to their house for an hour or so. A change of scene is often good for your child too, and someone else's toys are always more interesting. Toddler groups are also a great way of meeting other parents and of letting your children use up energy in a safe environment.

How to Enjoy Being a Dad

One of the best ways to enjoy being a dad is to spend time on your own with each of your children. All children love to have special 'Daddy time' and get very excited about spending quality time with you. The toddler years are a great time to forge this bond, as children are becoming less dependent on their mother for feeding and are often less clingy with her. Weekends are usually good for you as a dad to have quality time with your child, especially if you work long hours in the week. You'll be amazed how simple things such as taking your toddler with you to buy a newspaper or going down to the local park are a treat, just because she's spending time with you. If you have more than one child it's important to make space for one-to-one time with each child when you can and to make sure this is fairly distributed. Your other children could stay at home with Mum or go to see friends while you take one child out to do something special. As your children grow up you will be able to do more and more with them and share your own interests, whether it's going to a football match, camping, watching a film at the cinema or swimming.

Depending on your working pattern, it's great to spend time doing some of the daily routine with your child if you can. All families are different, but if you get home from work early enough you may be able to help with teatime, bathtime, storytime and bedtime routines. This is a lovely way to spend time with your child and can help you to wind down from the working day. However, it's important as parents to talk together about what your energy levels are like at the end of the day and decide who does what with the children. It can be hard as a father if you feel that you're handed a tired and cranky toddler as soon as you walk in the door, so keep talking to your partner about this. Some days, Mum will need to hand over to you if she's had a really tough day, so try to be as understanding as you can and then sit down together and have a glass of wine when you've finally got the children into bed.

Spending time together as a family can be especially enjoyable for fathers, as you and your partner can share your pride in your children when they're just happy being with you both. Try to make family time a priority, especially at weekends, when you may not have the pressure of work. Again, you don't have to go out and do expensive things; just having a relaxed breakfast or going for a walk can bring a sense of togetherness as a family. During the year there may be times when you can work flexible hours so that you can go to special events such as a party at the toddler group, sports day or a nativity play.

Balancing work and parenting can be a particular challenge for dads, as workplaces generally aren't as flexible for fathers – although I hope there will be continued progress on this. It's important not to feel guilty about the time you need to spend at work, especially if you have to work away from home. Your children will miss you, of course, but as long as you're able to have good quality time with them when you are at home their bond with you will be just as strong. Finding the balance that works best for you and your family is the most important thing. If you have a long commute, don't be afraid to ask whether you can work different hours or do some work from home if this suits your family life better. In the UK you have a legal right to *apply* for flexible working when you are a parent, although employers are not currently legally obliged to grant your request. You also have the right to take unpaid parental leave should you find that you need to take time off to support your family, especially in a time of crisis.

Recognizing the importance of your role will help you to enjoy being a father and will sustain you through the times when it's hard work. There are much higher expectations on fathers nowadays to be involved with caring for children, although at the same time I often notice in television programmes and advertisements that dads are portrayed as quite incompetent at life in general, while 'Supermum' is shown whizzing around her immaculate, gleaming home with spotless, contented children. I feel that fathers need to be encouraged that their role is absolutely invaluable and that they're doing a fantastic job in a culture which has moved on from fathers simply providing the bread on the table. As a dad, you're a tremendous role model for your child in the way you bring him up as well as in the way you provide support and back-up for your partner in parenting. Fathers are very important in helping to set the boundaries and providing consistent, loving discipline for children. It's natural for you to want to protect your children and to provide stability and security for your family. Your children will look up to you, and often children follow their father's lead in terms of core values such as what success means to you. Equally, children often love to have fun with their fathers, especially in rough-and-tumble play. As a dad it's a great enjoyment to help your children to have fun and laughter in their lives.

If you are separated from your partner, this can be very difficult, and at times you may feel you don't really know your children properly. Often you will only be seeing your children at weekends or during the holidays. Remember that you will always be 'Dad' to your children and nothing can take that away from you. What your child needs most from you as a father is your love and your time whenever you are together. Whatever the circumstances are that mean you are living away from your children, try to make the time you spend with them as normal as possible. Weekends and holidays don't need to be filled with expensive days out or presents, just with the same kinds of things that you did with them when you and your partner were living together. This will help to maintain the bond between you and build good memories for your children. As your children get older and are able to talk to you on the phone or send e-mails, it can be helpful for you to have contact with them during the week. Similarly, when the children stay with you it is good for them to keep in touch with their mum. As far as you possibly can, try to shield your children from any animosity between you and your partner, and don't engage in 'competitive' parenting. Instead, try to agree on the basics of how you both want to bring up your children.

Parenting Together

One of the best models for your child as he grows up is to see his parents working together in agreement and unity. This gives him great security as a child, but will also help him in adult life to approach relationships with openness and a desire to co-operate. As parents, family life is much easier if you're not pulling in different directions and you feel supported by one another. In the busyness of everyday life, it can be easy to just go on without talking together about any family problems. However, if you can make time to sit down together and talk about how things are going with the children, whether you feel you're having enough time together as a family and how you're going to sort out any problems, it can help to bring you back together as a couple. Make time as well to share the good things and the hopes and dreams you have for your family; after a good day there's nothing like sitting back and having a smile about the things you've enjoyed as a family. It's good to tell each other how proud you are of the job you're both doing as parents, in the good times and the tricky ones too.

No family is perfect, and there will be times when you simply don't agree with one another and you don't feel very 'together' in your parenting. Bringing up children can be a very stressful job at times, and you'll almost certainly have moments when you feel incredibly cross with each other. I often find that one of the common flashpoints for disagreement between parents is disciplining the children and stating what the boundaries are. When you do disagree, try your hardest not to undermine or criticize what the other parent is doing in front of your child. When we bring one another down as parents, it's surprising how quickly this can cause children to be disrespectful to both parents or not listen to what they are saying. Even young toddlers will pick up on an angry tone of voice, and though they won't understand why you are cross with each other they will be affected. As far as possible try to discuss areas of disagreement when your child is in bed.

Obviously we can't and wouldn't want to shield our children from everything that is negative as that would be unrealistic, and children need to grow up with a balanced outlook on life. If you find you have been angry with each other in front of your child, the best thing to do is to make sure that she sees you resolving things and to reassure her that it wasn't her fault. Equally, if you have been angry with your child or have had to reprimand her, it is important to make sure she knows that the matter is resolved and that you still love her. This will help your child to grow up knowing how to do this in her relationships too.

Keeping a Strong Relationship

The reality of everyday family life can bring pressures and tensions that at times seem insurmountable, and there are days when we feel we don't even like our partner! These feelings are quite normal from time to time but do not indicate that we should give up on our relationship. I am a strong believer in marriage; I feel it is a commitment that we should take seriously as a society. I say this even in the light of my own personal experience of divorce and remarriage. The very act of marriage is in itself a promise to stick together 'no matter what', which is witnessed by family and friends around you. When times are hard, which at some stage they will be, you can look back on the vows of commitment you made to one another. I find one of the most moving things about the traditional marriage vows is that we promise to be together 'in sickness and in health, for richer, for poorer, for better, for worse'. Marriage vows often also include the witnesses, who promise to do 'everything they can to uphold and support you in your marriage'. This provides an amazing base for family life. I read an article recently about the widow of Steve Irwin, the well-known Australian crocodile hunter. When she was interviewed shortly after his death she said through her tears, 'I've lost my prince.' They must have had a very special relationship for her to see him as her prince and best friend. Often in the media we see bitterness, insults and animosity within marriages presented as the norm. Yet marriage can and should be a wonderful relationship of trust and tenderness, in which you cherish each other and feel secure in your love for one another.

We need to work at our relationships; they don't just happen! I remember my mother saying to me in the early years of my marriage, 'You each need to give 100 per cent to your marriage, then it will work.' Your children will thrive when they see you as a couple showing love and affection for each other, so even when you are not feeling like it, remember that your children need to see you loving each other and loving them too. Children who grow up in a loving, caring environment will in general be more stable and find relationships easier in adult life. Although this isn't a book on marriage and relationships, I want to share some tips that I hope will build up your relationship as you parent together:

- *Listen to each other.*
- *Enable your partner to unburden his or her heart without fear.*
- *Encourage each other as parents; tell your partner what a great job he or she is doing.*
- *Try not to undermine your partner in parenting.*
- *Love life and find ways of making your relationship fun.*
- *Laugh at your mistakes; don't let things get too serious.*

One of the things that can put pressure on your relationship is if children go through a phase when they seem to prefer one parent to the other. Toddlers often go through a clingy stage with one parent, and this is perfectly normal. The other parent can feel very upset, bruised and left out by this. As a couple, talk it through and try not to take it personally if you are the parent feeling left out. It can make things worse if you make a fuss about it, so patiently and gradually encourage your child to do more things with both parents. This stage will pass, but it's important not to let it come between you as a couple.

It is important to have shared interests as a couple and to do things without the children. When the children are in bed it can be tempting to plonk yourself down in front of the television, but this can be valuable time together. It can be helpful to do different things in the evenings; you could try putting photo albums together, reading bits of the newspaper to each other, researching your family genealogy on the computer or anything that interests you as a couple. If you're able, try to have one night a week when you can go out for a meal or a drink and leave the children with a babysitter. You could try setting up a babysitting circle, where friends with children babysit for each other so that it doesn't cost you anything. This is quite a good way to do it especially if you don't have any family around to help out. Evenings together can help you to keep your lines of communication open and to talk through any issues that have come up during the week. Often going out can make it easier to talk than staying at home.

On special occasions such as anniversaries, it can be a treat to have a night away somewhere without the children. When you are ready to do this, make sure that your child's carer knows him really well so that you feel comfortable leaving him and don't spend the whole night worrying. As the toddler years go on you may feel comfortable having a few days away, leaving your toddler with family or friends. This was something we didn't do as our children were growing up, and we now regret not having done so. I believe that children benefit from having a few nights away with family or friends. Having said that, you do need to know that your children are ready for this, especially if you haven't left them overnight on many occasions before.

Helping Siblings to Get Along Together

It is a joy to see siblings laughing and playing together, obviously enjoying each other's company. However, as parents we know that this doesn't always happen; one minute they can be playing well and the next it sounds as though World War Three has broken out! We need to encourage our children to be fair and play well together and to watch out for each other's needs. One thing that helps to prevent conflict between our children is being careful to treat each child equally, and not showing any favouritism. With young children, you'll find you have to show siblings how to share their toys and to make sure that each child feels they have had an equal turn. This will be tiring at times, but you are teaching your children important lessons about getting on with others and co-operating.

Even though your children will battle with each other sometimes, a great thing about having siblings is that they can learn to care for one another in a special way. It is a good idea to encourage older children to help out with the younger ones right from the start, when a new baby is born (see Chapter 11).

Help your children to show physical affection to one another; for example, if a young child falls over the older one can help her up and give her a cuddle and comfort her. Encouraging your children to say sorry to one another and 'kiss it better' if they've hurt each other is part of this special sibling bond.

In families, each child needs to feel special, valued and loved, and it can be quite tricky as a parent to make sure this happens. When possible, it is great if all the children can have some one-to-one time with you doing something that they enjoy. When there are babies or young toddlers around, older children will need to feel that their space and toys are protected from little ones spoiling the game. You could try having a baby-free zone in your older child's bedroom where he can retreat with his toys. However, it's important also to encourage your older child to be tolerant and play with his younger brothers or sisters at times, getting involved in what they are doing. Praise your older child when he plays well with his younger siblings, as this will encourage him and make him feel grown up and a 'big boy'. However, don't expect your older child to always be minding the younger ones, as this isn't fair on him. One of the best things to do if siblings are getting tense with each other is to do something together outdoors as a family, such as going to the park or the playground. This often seems to diffuse things quickly and will encourage your children to bond and play together.

Brothers and sisters often have fantastic fun playing rough-and-tumble games with one another, and it's important not to discourage them from doing this. However, sometimes you will find that your children get a bit overexcited or games turn into genuine conflict. If any of your children start hitting, biting or spitting in rough play you must intervene, as this is not acceptable in any way (see the section on managing behaviour in Chapter 3). Young children often enjoy launching into each other, but watch them as again you may need to intervene, especially if the smaller one is getting bashed up! Often, though, children sort it out by themselves, and holding back as a parent can help your children to develop healthy ways of playing and resolving things together.

How to Enjoy Being a Grandparent

Just before I came to write this chapter my husband and I had a holiday in France with all our family – thirteen of us altogether. It was wonderful being with the five grandchildren, ranging in age from nine years down to seven months. We had fun with them all, and we felt we were building very special memories for them, which the older ones would never forget. While we were on holiday I cooked the children pancakes for a special treat for supper one evening, and our little five-year-old grandson said, 'Gan Gan, you always cook us such lovely food!' Doing something very simple for them gave them such pleasure. I have found, as our grandchildren have got older, that they are fascinated when they understand that my husband and I are their mummy or daddy's parents. There was a special joy for us in seeing all the young cousins playing together and watching that bond developing between the next generation. There has been a great sense of fulfilment in seeing this legacy of love and relationship in the wider family.

As a grandparent, never underestimate the effect that you have on your grandchildren's lives. Your love will bring a huge sense of security and stability to them, and you can have great fun with them too. You can bring a different aspect to their life, as you may have more time than parents for games, reading stories, playing and just talking. You don't have the ultimate responsibility for bringing them up and so there can be more freedom to have fun, and less of the worry that you've already gone through as a parent. As grandparents or even great-grandparents, you will remember a very different society from today and this can be a huge benefit to your grandchildren. As they grow up, they'll be interested to hear your stories about what your childhood was like and you can help them to understand how the world has changed.

As grandparents you have a special role to play, and it will help you to enjoy your role more if you try hard not to undermine what the parents are doing with their young children. It is always easy to think that we know best, but remember that each generation brings up their children slightly differently from the generation before. This can sometimes be hard for grandparents to see and we can find it difficult not to intervene, but don't give advice unless you are asked. It can be easy to spoil a good family relationship by interfering when our comments are not needed. You can build a much stronger relationship with your own children if you encourage them in what they are doing with their children and wait for them to come to you as and when they need help.

If you're not involved with day-to-day childcare and the grandchildren are coming to visit or stay with you, it's a good idea to get a sense from the parents of what things are allowed. For example, find out if it is all right to let the grandchildren watch a bit more television than usual or have a treat like a chocolate biscuit or an ice cream. All these sorts of things build happy memories for grandchildren, and they learn that it is fun to be with Granny and Grandpa because they do exciting things there. On the flip-side, you may well find that parents have quite different house rules from your own. If you don't want your grandchildren to put their feet on the sofa or have their tea in the sitting room, this is perfectly fine. Children soon get used to a different set of rules at Granny and Grandpa's house, and this is very healthy for them. Often your own children will parent in quite different ways from you, and so the grandchildren's behaviour may not be quite as you would like it to be. It can be easy to show favouritism to one particular grandchild, especially if they are more similar to you in nature. Sadly, this can cause problems for years, so if you are feeling like this take a look at yourself and make a positive step to spend time with all your grandchildren and accept them for who they are. If you are really struggling with a grandchild's behaviour, find a quiet time to talk to the parents about it rather than avoiding contact.

If you're a grandparent who is involved in regular childcare, you will probably find that you and your children disagree on some practical aspects of how to bring up the grandchildren. The most important thing is to talk these things through together to diffuse any possible argument. Try to be as flexible as you can and find a balance that works for all of you, keeping in mind the children's needs as your priority. I feel there is a huge expectation on grandparents to help out with childcare today, and sometimes this can be too much to manage. Remember that you will tire more quickly than you did with your own young family, and don't be afraid to tell your children if you are feeling overloaded. However, I have received many letters from clients whose parents help with childcare and all say that they couldn't do it without the grandparents, who are a wonderful support and help in many ways.

Closing Thoughts

I hope that this chapter has given you some ideas to help you enjoy the tiring but incredibly rewarding toddler years. The fun times that you have with your child in these years are never wasted and help to build a strong foundation for her as she grows up. However, when you have had a frazzled day, try to remember that none of us is the perfect parent and that you can always put it behind you and start afresh tomorrow.

CHAPTER 13

Your Toddler's Spiritual and Emotional Needs

As parents it's easy to focus on meeting our child's physical needs. In the toddler years we can get very worried about whether we're doing all the practical things right, such as potty training, helping our child to eat well, managing tantrums and sleep problems – the list goes on. I believe that it is important to remember that children have an emotional and spiritual side that needs nurturing just as much. Often we can be constantly rushing around, forgetting to stop and 'smell the roses' with our child. We need to make time to tell our children how much we love them and how precious they are. Being a mother and a grandmother and having looked after countless children over the years, I have learnt that all children thrive on knowing that they are deeply and unconditionally loved. This is the key to our child's emotional and spiritual wellbeing.

I write as a Christian and I hope that wherever you are in your own faith journey, this chapter will be an inspiration and an encouragement to you. The Bible says that we as humans are made in the image of God, which is a staggering thought. I believe that God's very nature is love. The Greek word for God's love is *agape*, which means a self-giving love that perseveres even when we turn away or do things wrong. As a Christian I believe that God knows our struggles with life and how often we feel failure and guilt as parents, and yet he still goes on giving us unconditional love. Many of us feel a new connection with this selfless love when we have children. We may be tested to our limits by our toddlers at times and yet we still love them passionately and want to protect them.

Love is patient and kind. Love is not jealous or boastful or proud or rude. It does not demand its own way. It is not irritable, and it keeps

no record of being wronged. It does not rejoice about injustice but rejoices whenever the truth wins out. Love never gives up, never loses faith, is always hopeful, and endures through every circumstance.

1 Corinthians 13:4–7

How Do I Show My Child Love?

Young children may not be able to fully understand when we say 'I love you', but there are many ways that we as parents can express love to our children in both words and actions. The simplest, and yet the most important to our child, is that we spend time with him. It's interesting that toddlers often play up when they don't feel they've got enough of our attention. Sometimes breaking off what we're doing to spend a few minutes with our child can be enough to help him feel happy and secure again. The main ways in which children understand love are through our time, our words and our physical affection. All of these things build up trust between you and your child, which will help you to feel secure through the challenging times of family life.

Quality Time with Your Child

Spending one-to-one time with your child can be difficult, as family life is often hectic. However, it's important to find moments to enjoy simply being with your child, as these early years pass very quickly and before you know where you are she's at school all day. Whether you're at home with children or working full- or part-time, try to carve out some time when you can just chat with your child or play together. The evening routine can be an ideal time to relax with your child, whether you are chatting to her while she has tea, bathing her, playing a game or reading a story together before bed.

Your child will enjoy it if he can be involved in what you're doing; something as simple as letting him help you with the washing-up can show him that you love being in his company, and you can both have fun at the same time. When you are playing with your child you can try getting on the floor with him at his level, as this helps him to know that you're joining in with what he is doing (see Chapter 7 for lots of ideas on things to do together). Weekends can be good for spending some more extended time together with your children just enjoying things that they like to do, such as going to a playground or park. I always say that the housework can wait!

Affirmation and Encouragement

Even as adults, we know the powerful effect that words can have on how we feel about ourselves. A well-timed compliment or a word of encouragement can be just the thing to give us a lift on a stressful day. In the same way, children love to hear affirming words from us as parents that convey how proud we are of them and how special they are and that we love them no matter what. Even before your child can understand what you're saying, your tone of voice when you say affirming words will give her great comfort and make her feel secure, as she knows you're pleased with her. By speaking to your child in love you are teaching her to speak loving words to others too.

A good rule of thumb for affirming your child is to praise him simply for who he is. It's very important for children to hear phrases such as 'You are such a wonderful boy' or 'You're my precious girl', which don't necessarily relate to specific 'good behaviour'. This helps children to know that they're loved unconditionally. Of course it's important too to encourage your child when he behaves well. Being specific helps your child to understand what you are praising him for, so it's good to say, for example, 'It was very kind when you shared your toy' rather than just 'Good boy'. Talking to your child like this can take some practice, especially if you didn't grow up in an environment where feelings were shared very much or you weren't affirmed yourself. It's important not to feel guilty if you find it difficult to praise your child; perhaps you could try to talk it through with your partner and think about your own childhood.

Physical Affection

Cuddling and holding your child often comes very naturally in the baby stage, but it may be harder to have much 'cuddly time' with toddlers, as they are more active and will sometimes wriggle away from hugs to go and play. Try not to take it personally if this happens; your child will snuggle up with you again as she gets older. Moments of physical touch such as holding your child's hand or stroking her head and face will help her to know that you're still there when she needs you for physical comfort. You may have been brought up to be very comfortable with physical expressions of love, or your own family may not have been very demonstrative. It's a good idea to talk this through as parents and decide how you want to be with your own children. If physical affection brings up difficult memories for you, it's important to talk about this with someone you can trust, and you may want to seek counselling.

Here are some ways in which you can show physical affection to your toddler:

- *hugging him in the morning when you first lift him out of his cot or bed*
- *cuddling him to comfort him when he falls over*
- *snuggling up together while reading a book or watching television (although toddlers may not sit on your knee for long!)*
- *stroking your child's head before he goes to sleep*
- *tickling and rough-and-tumble playing*
- *singing songs with touch, such as 'Round and round the garden'.*

What About the Days When It All Goes Wrong?

Life isn't always perfect, and there are days when everything feels like a battle with your toddler. When you get tired or are under pressure for whatever reason, these days can feel even worse. Equally, there are days when you will be too busy to give lots of attention to your child and it's a case of just making it to bedtime. Try not to worry, and don't feel guilty; there are times when we don't get it right and feel a failure, but there is always the chance to start again the next day.

As parents, you may get angry and shout or even swear at your children, but it's important to remember that words can deeply affect a child. If children regularly hear unkind words about themselves such as 'You are a horrible boy', this can dent their self-esteem. As the adults, you need to be ready to say sorry and reassure your child that you still love *him*, even if his *behaviour* has been naughty.

Building Special Memories

As adults, our fondest childhood memories are often of the simple things we did regularly with our parents, such as going to a weekly football match, going for walks, cooking or gardening together. Think about the things from your own childhood that make you say, 'Do you remember when we used to…?' and you'll often find they are quite simple pleasures. It's a great joy as a parent to begin to build these kinds of memories into your children's lives. We live in a busier world in general than our own parents, so don't feel guilty if there is less time for simple pleasures; just enjoy them with your children when you can.

Often our most vivid memories from childhood are of special birthday parties, holidays and family gatherings. I think it's important to celebrate big events like birthdays if you possibly can, as the toddler years go by so quickly. However, it doesn't have to involve an expensive or flashy party; a simple gathering with a few friends, a cake and a party tea is all that toddlers need. It's lovely for older children to look back on photos of birthday celebrations and to see the different cakes they had when they were little. Family holidays can also be great times to build memories together, and they don't have to cost a lot of money. Just to go away for a few days can do you good and recharge your batteries. Staying with friends or family is often a good way to have a holiday when your children are young. One thing to bear in mind on family holidays is that your children will enjoy just spending time with you, so don't feel that every day has to be action-packed.

I heard recently about a family keeping a 'treasure box' to hold memories of special times, and I think this is a wonderful idea. This could be as simple as a shoebox containing special photos, your child's first painting, some clothes from when they were tiny, and maybe records such as their annual height measurement. You could try taking a family photo every year to add to the collection. You will find as your children grow up that they love to see these special things. One thing we did with our own children was to record their chattering at mealtimes when they were young, and it was hilarious to listen to this when they were grown up.

Spirituality in a Toddler's Life

How vital it is to fill our children's memories with natural beauty so that they have a 'bank account' to draw on during ugly times in later life.

Jennifer Rees Larcombe, *Journey into God's Heart*

We all have times in life when we do, see or hear things that make us feel good. We could call them our 'soul' times; the times that make us tick and bring a smile to our face. It can be just looking at our children when they are peacefully asleep; it may be experiencing nature – the trees, the hills, the sea, flowers in the hedgerows, birdsong; or it may be appreciating the arts – viewing a painting, listening to a piece of music, hearing a choir sing or looking at a piece of sculpture. Being uplifted by nature or the arts can make us feel more aware of our spiritual side, somehow closer to God. As adults we need these times and it is important to encourage our children to experience this too, to explore the wonder of the world and the arts and music. I believe that people are much more open to spirituality today than they were when I was a young mother, and I am thrilled that young parents are happy to talk about these issues.

One of the ways to build spirituality into family life is to take time to explore and wonder at nature. Most children love going for walks, and this is a good opportunity for you to share nature with them. If you are in a park or a country lane, show them the flowers, trees and bushes and let them smell the flowers if you can. The different seasons bring new plants, flowers and colours and it's wonderful to help your child to connect with this natural rhythm of change. Listen to the birds singing; stop and let her see a bird flying by; feed the ducks in the park. These times are very special, and you are building an awareness and appreciation of beauty in the world.

Over the years one thing I have learnt is that children need times of stillness, peace, quiet and even contemplation. You may wonder about this, especially if you have a very active toddler. Reflecting on the day and saying 'thank you' to God can be a natural thing to do at bedtime when you are tucking your child in and kissing him goodnight. It is a time when you can talk about all the things you have done in the day, gather them together, however simple they are, and offer them as a prayer of thanksgiving to God. I have found that praying with children if they wake in the night with a bad dream helps them to settle again. You can take your child onto your lap and cuddle him while you pray; this can be very calming and reassuring. I feel this is a precious thing to do with your child, even if you are not sure that you believe in God yourself.

Here is a simple child's prayer that may help you to get started:

> Dear God, thank you so much for all the lovely things we have done today [you could name some]. Thank you for Mummy and Daddy and for [name siblings, grandparents, friends]. Please give us a good night's sleep. Amen.

If you are wondering about Christianity you could try going to a family service, which most churches hold at least once a month. These services are usually informal and child-friendly. You may also find comfort from going to a loving, caring church where you feel 'part of the family', especially if you live far from relatives or have been through hard times. Many churches have Sunday school or children's activities, and children often make good friends there. At church your child will probably learn songs and Bible stories as well as playing games and doing craft activities. There are plenty of colourful Bible storybooks available if you want to read these at home. Similarly, worship CDs for children teach about God and his love in a way that children can understand and engage with.

When Life Hurts

Come to me, all you who are weary and burdened, and I will give you rest.

Matthew 11:28

Most people will face hurt and hardship at some time in their lives, whether it is separation, divorce, unemployment, debt, illness or the death of a family member. Any of these situations will deeply affect family life. What do we do and where do we turn when life hurts? Are there any answers, and how do we find peace in this situation? In my own life, I feel I have known the love of God in amazing ways on some of the darkest days. When I have been through very difficult times, I found sometimes I couldn't pray, but it was wonderful to have the support of loving praying friends, and it felt as though they were carrying me through. My faith has not prevented pain or provided easy answers, but it has given me a hope that sustained me, as I knew I was never alone.

In difficult times your distress is bound to rub off on your child, and your instinct will be to protect her from the situation that you find yourself in, but sadly the reality of life is that you may not be able to. Remember that your child probably feels her world is being tipped upside-down too, so try to explain to her gently what's happening so that she feels safe. Whatever you are going through, try to keep your child's days as normal as possible and maybe ask another family member or close friend to help. If one parent is seriously ill, it is important that the other parent is able to support your child as much as possible, again getting family help in if you are not coping. If there is a death in the wider family a young toddler will probably not understand why the grown-ups are upset and may just carry on as normal. However, the death of a parent will obviously affect a child of any age very deeply and you will need lots of help and support. As a bereaved parent, it's important to have professional support for yourself and your children (for example, from the UK organization Cruse Bereavement Care) to help you through the process of grieving.

Closing Thoughts

As we come to the close of this chapter and of the book, I hope that you have found comfort and help in it. My desire is that you will enjoy parenting your children through the practical and emotional care you give them day by day, and find it amazingly fulfilling and exciting as you see them grow and mature. My prayer is that you will know God's touch of love and faithfulness on your lives as you journey along the path of family life together.

Appendix: Flexible Routine Charts

Many parents have asked me to set out some guide timings for routines, which adapt as children grow. I hope the charts on the following pages will be a helpful guide but remember that these timings are flexible to suit the needs of your family. I've set out timings on the hour but of course this doesn't mean that you need to start each activity on the dot.

Guideline Timings for One-year-olds

Time	Activity	Notes
6.00	Wake up	Wake any time from about 6.00 to 7.30. May still have a feed on waking
7.00		
8.00	Breakfast	
9.00	Play time	
10.00	Nap	Nap any time from 10. May sleep for up to two hours
11.00		
12.00	Lunch	Lunch any time from about 12 to 1.30
1.00		
2.00	Play or going out	
3.00	Short nap	Nap often around 20 mins. Can be in buggy
4.00		
5.00	Teatime	Early tea from 4.30 if you prefer
6.00	Bathtime	
7.00	Bedtime	May still have evening feed. Settle to sleep any time from about 6.30

Guideline Timings for Two-year-olds

Time	Activity	Notes
6.00		
7.00	Wake up	Some toddlers wake earlier, but if he is happy playing in his cot you don't need to get him up
8.00	Breakfast	
9.00	Play or going out	
10.00		
11.00	Nap	Will usually nap for about one to one and a half hours
12.00	Lunch	Lunch any time between 12 and 1.30. Nap and lunch are interchangeable if your toddler prefers to eat before sleeping
1.00		
2.00	Play, going out or activities at home	Most two-year-olds don't need a further nap unless very tired
3.00		Can nap in car or buggy if you are out
4.00		
5.00	Teatime	
6.00	Bathtime	
7.00	Bedtime	

Guideline Timings for Three-year-olds

Time	Activity	Notes
6.00		
7.00	Wake up	
8.00	Breakfast	
9.00	May go to nursery	Most three-year-olds don't need a daytime nap, but after nursery or preschool she may be tired and need a sleep
10.00		
11.00		
12.00		If she needs a nap this can be before or after lunch
1.00	Lunch	Lunch any time between 12 and 2
2.00		
3.00	Play or going out	
4.00		
5.00	Teatime	
6.00	Bathtime	
7.00	Bedtime	

Combining a Toddler's and a Baby's Routine

Time	Toddler	Baby (0–3 months)
6.00		Feed*
7.00	Wake up	Wakeful time or back to sleep in cot
8.00	Breakfast	
9.00	Go to preschool or nursery	Can sleep in car or buggy (or play time if toddler is at home)
10.00		Feed*
11.00	Collect from preschool or nursery	Sleep in car or buggy if needed or nap in cot from 11.30, or when you get home
12.00	Lunch	
1.00	Nap	
2.00		Feed
3.00	Play time or walk	Sleep in cot or buggy if you have a walk
4.00		
5.00	Teatime	Snack feed if needed**
6.00	Bathtime	Bath before or with toddler. Feed at about 6.30
7.00	Settle to bed	Bedtime***

*During these feeds, try to put your feet up and have a quiet restful time with your baby.

**If you find your baby is unsettled at teatime, try giving a small feed to settle and then the rest of the feed after bathtime.

***Toddler may need to settle before baby. If so, lay baby on your bed or take him into toddler's room while you settle toddler.

Index